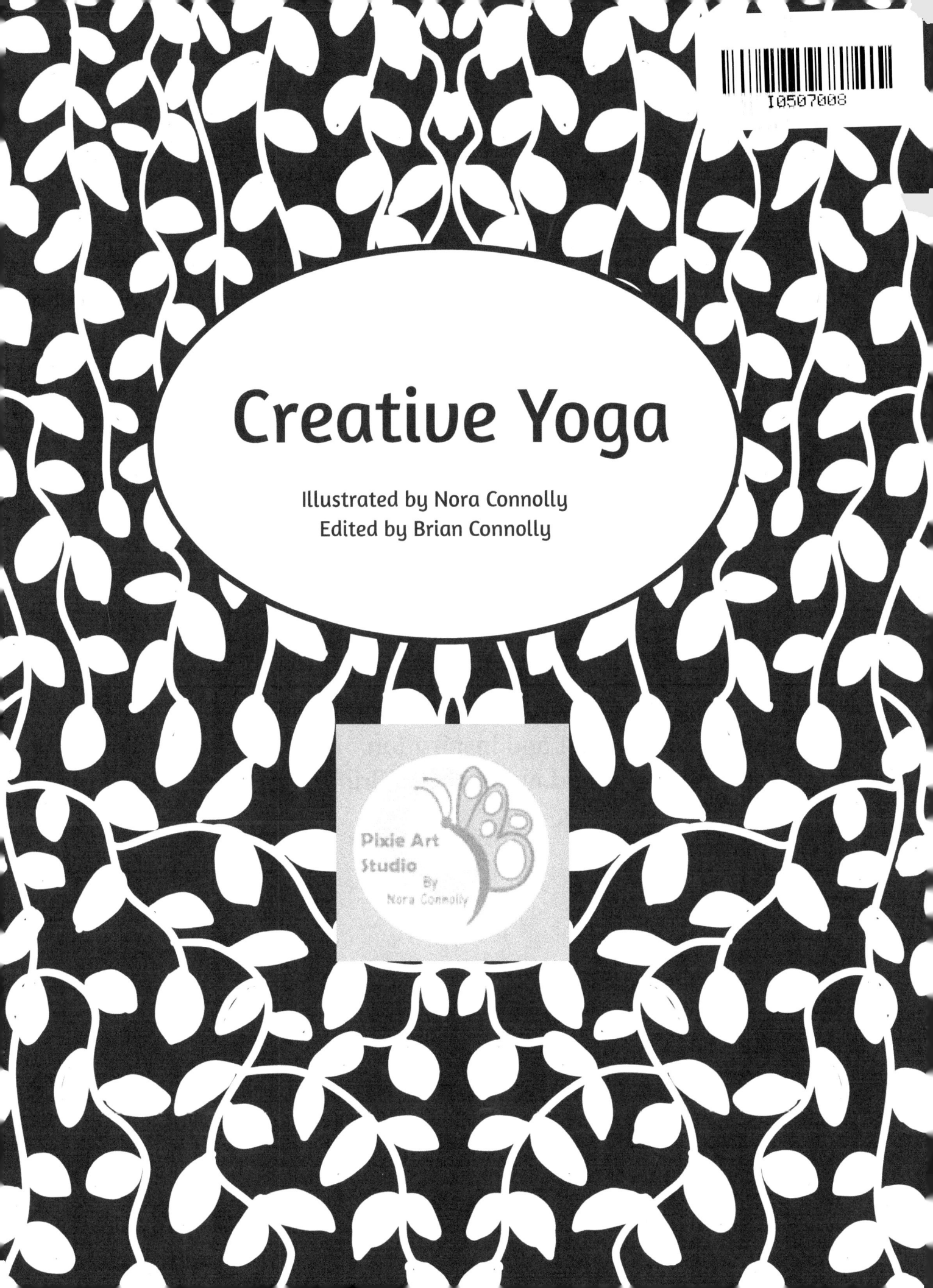

Creative Yoga

Illustrated by Nora Connolly
Edited by Brian Connolly

Dear reader,

    Many thanks for choosing my book. I hope that this book brings you much peace and relaxation. The purpose of "Creative Yoga" is to create a space where you can shift your mind and focus to a more placid and content state. This can be done by coloring in the many illustrations throughout the book. Alongside each image is a quote to reflect on as you color away.

    - Nora C.

+ + + + +

I would like to dedicate this book to a few people in my life who have had an indelible impact on me. Their unconditional love and support has been my greatest comfort and inspiration. To my Mom, my brother Alex, and my husband Brian, this one's for you! Thank you.

Copyright © 2021 - Pixie Art Studio
All rights reserved.
ISBN# 9798598083635
www.pixieartstudio.com

Buddha

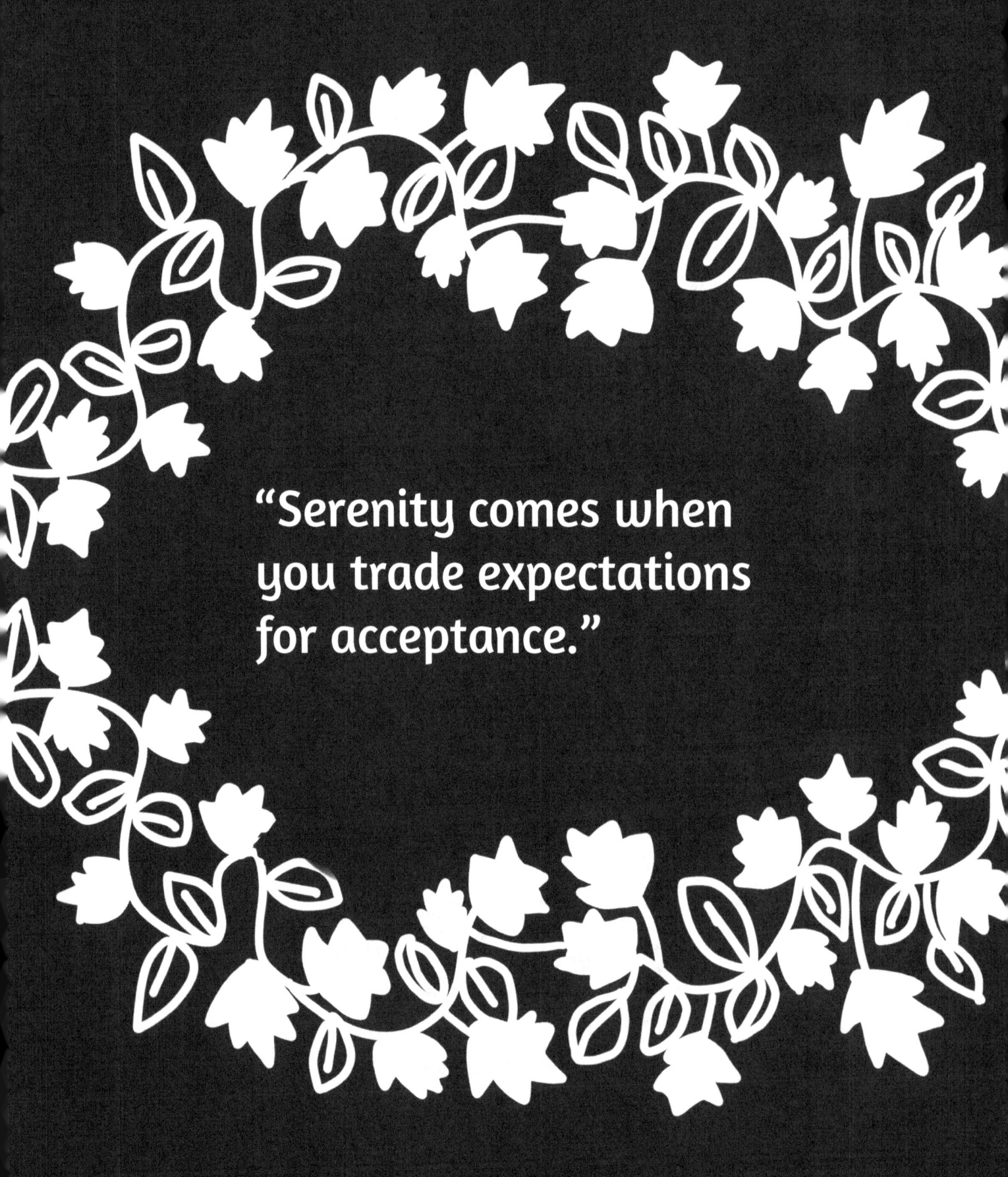

"Serenity comes when you trade expectations for acceptance."

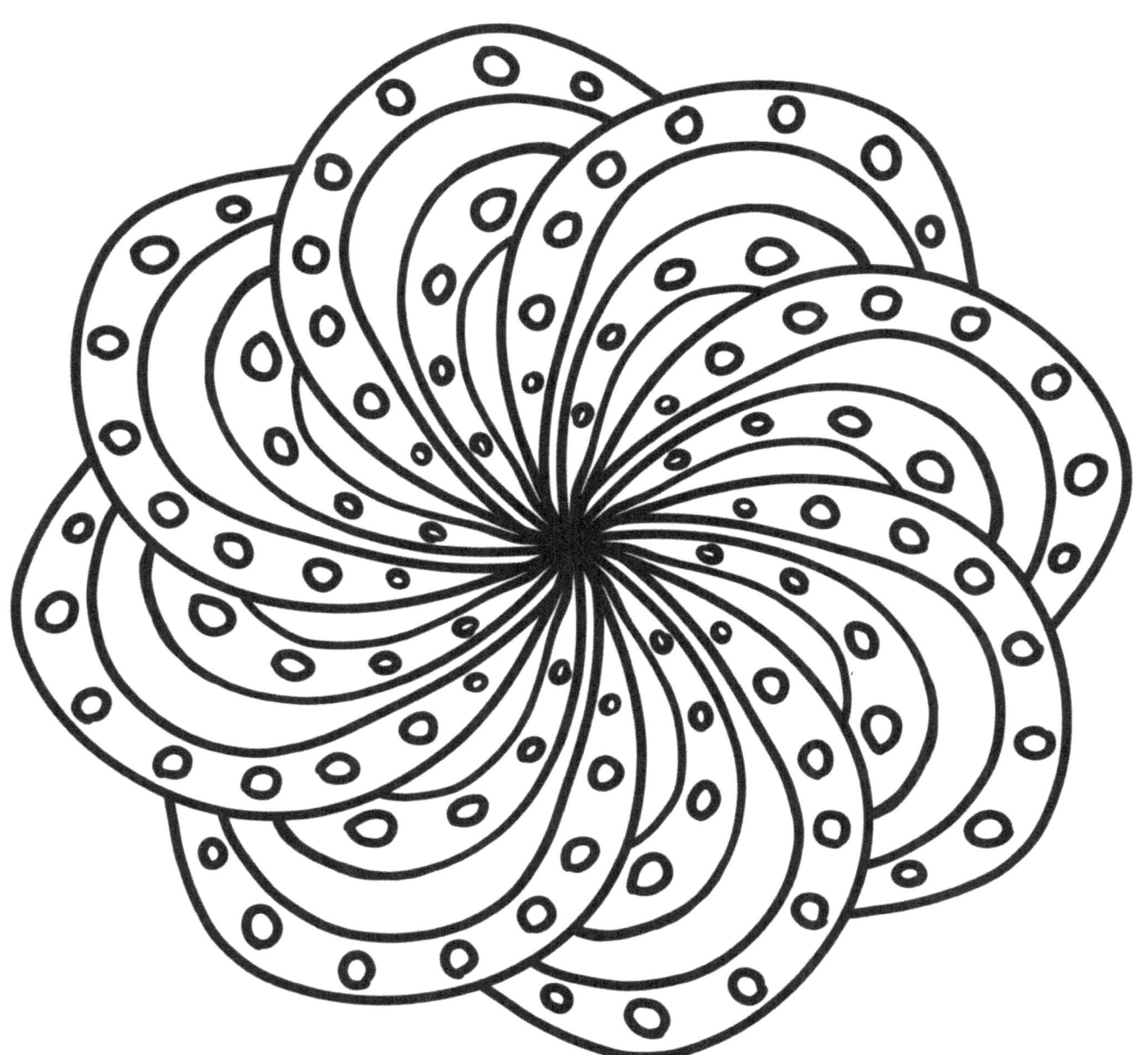

Inhale in

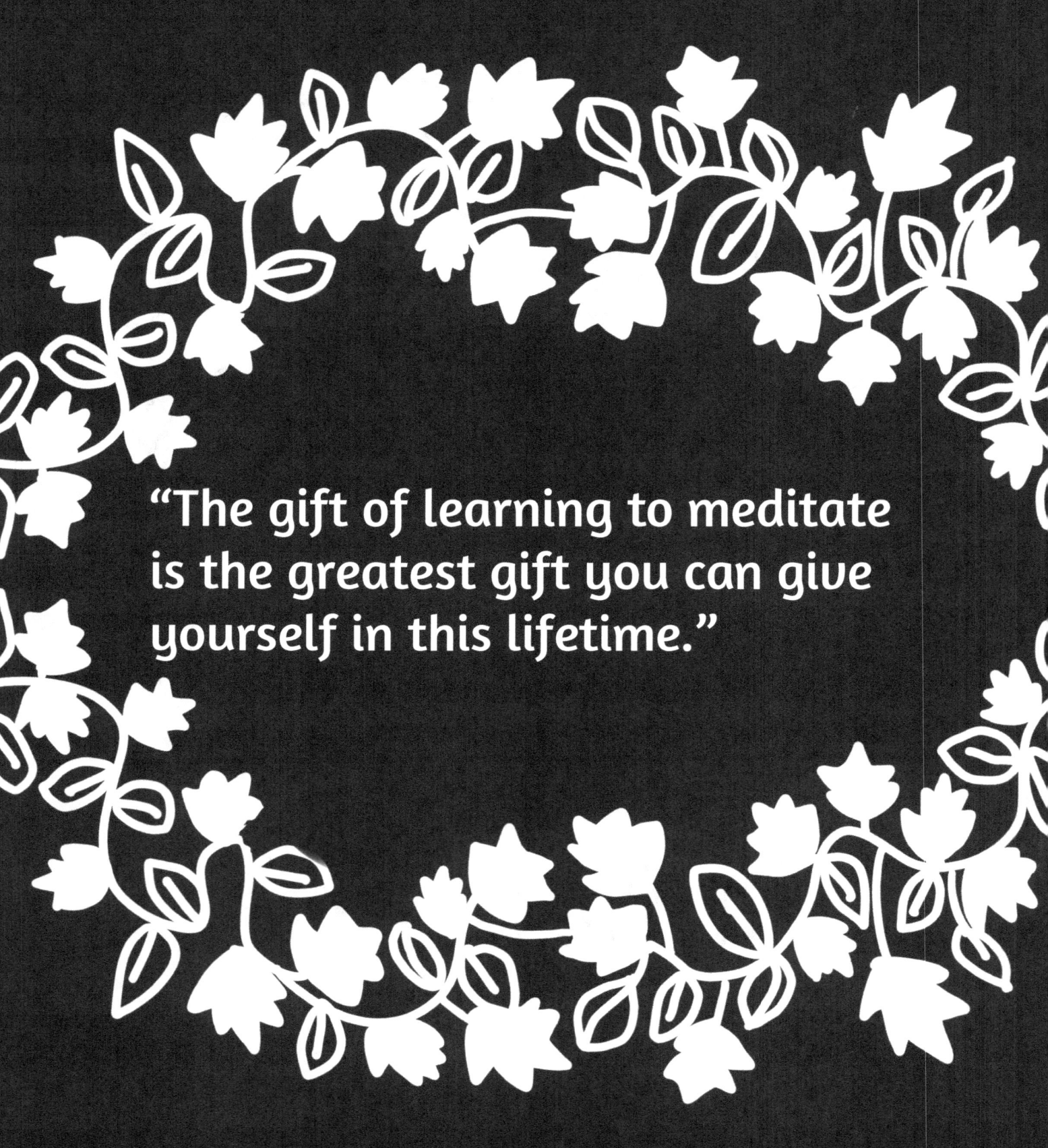

"The gift of learning to meditate is the greatest gift you can give yourself in this lifetime."

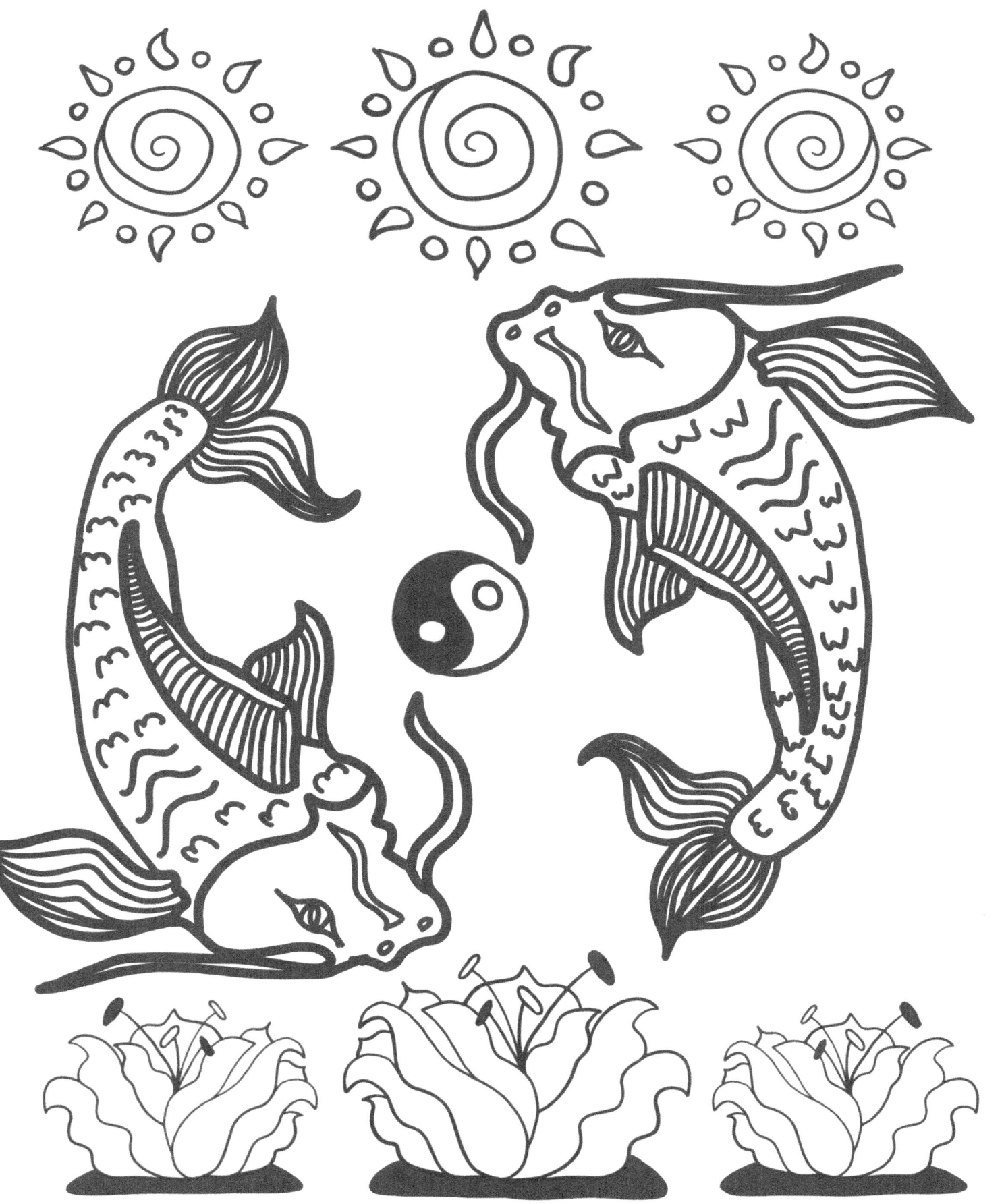

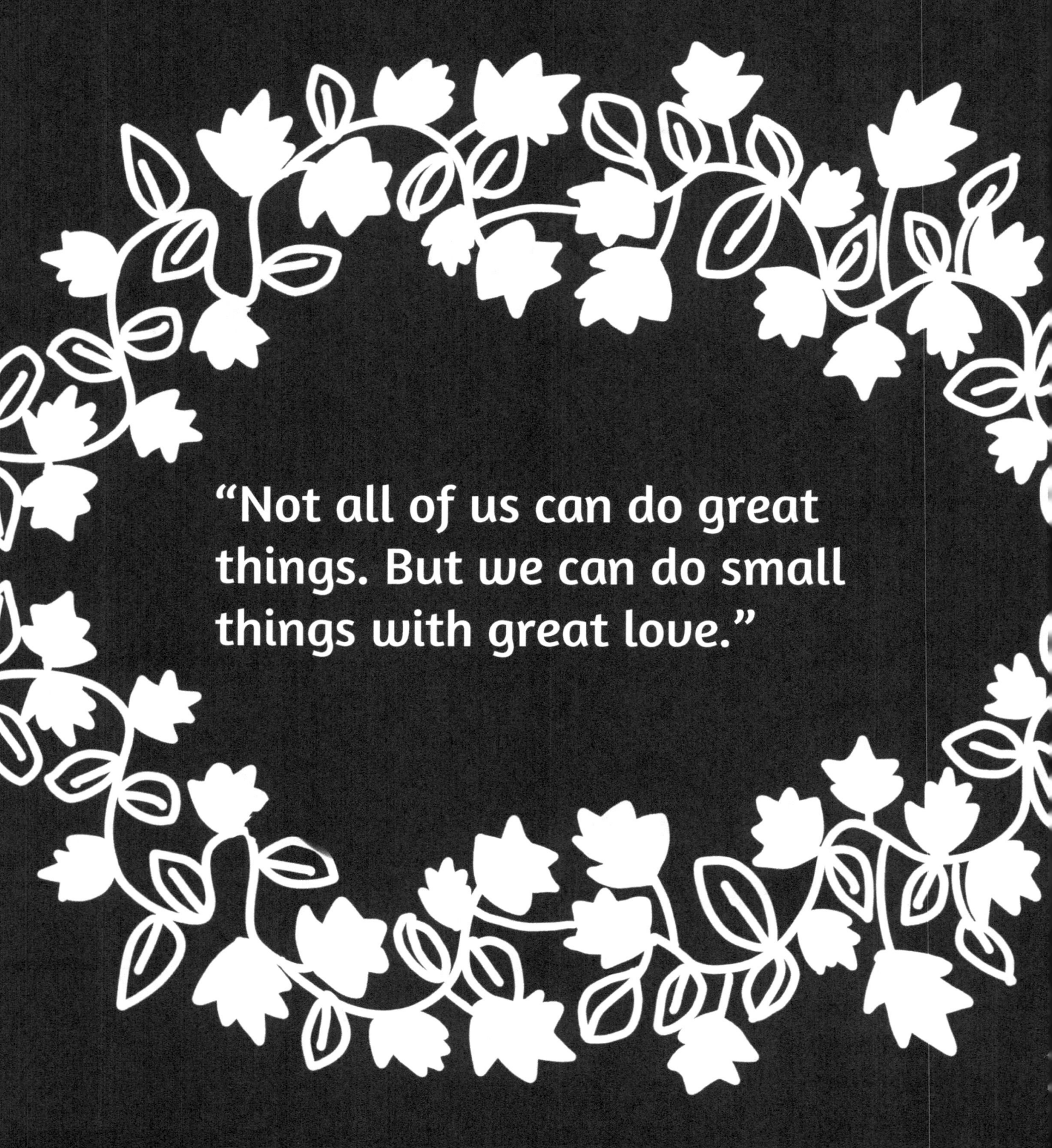

"Not all of us can do great things. But we can do small things with great love."

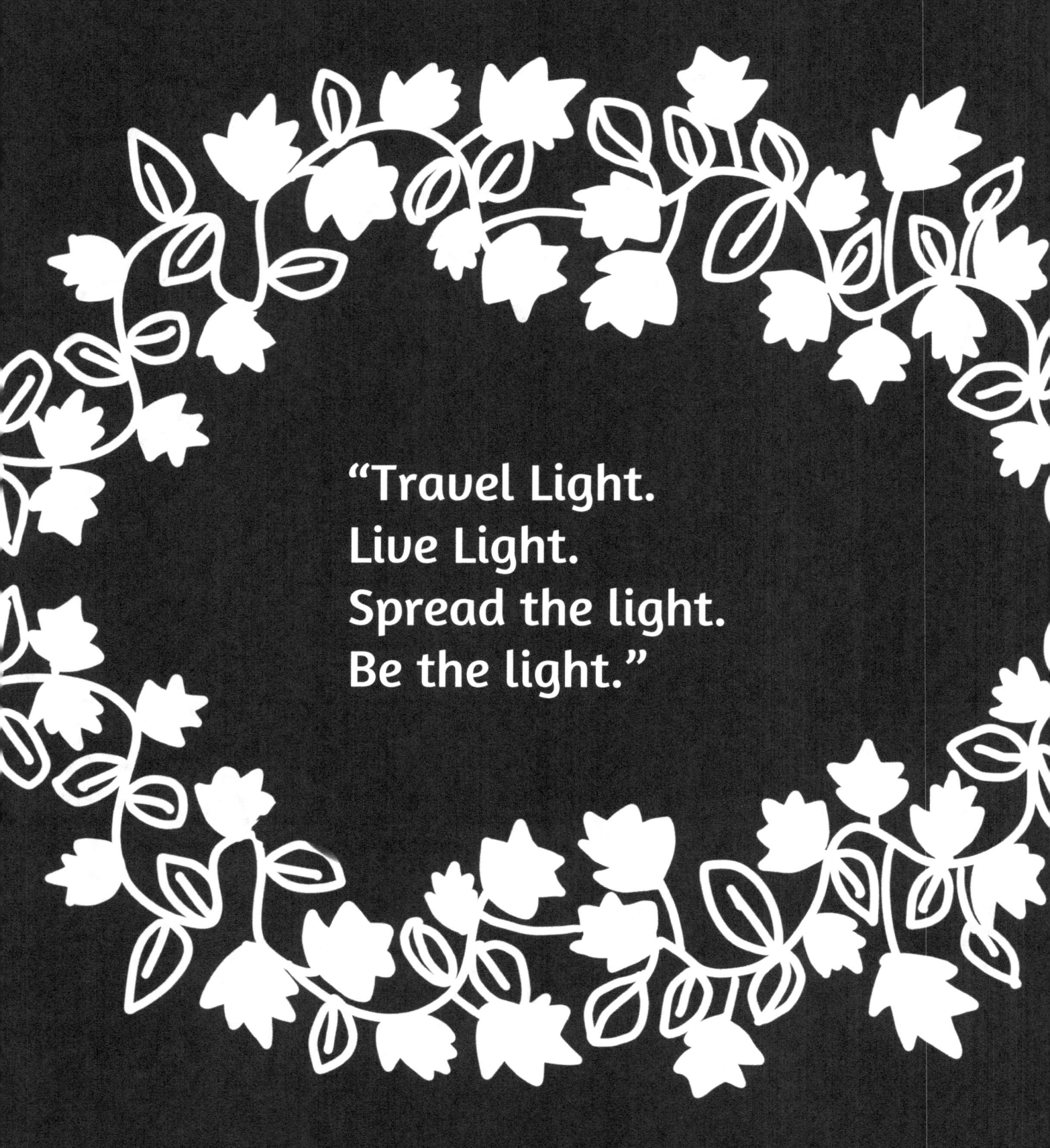

"Travel Light.
Live Light.
Spread the light.
Be the light."

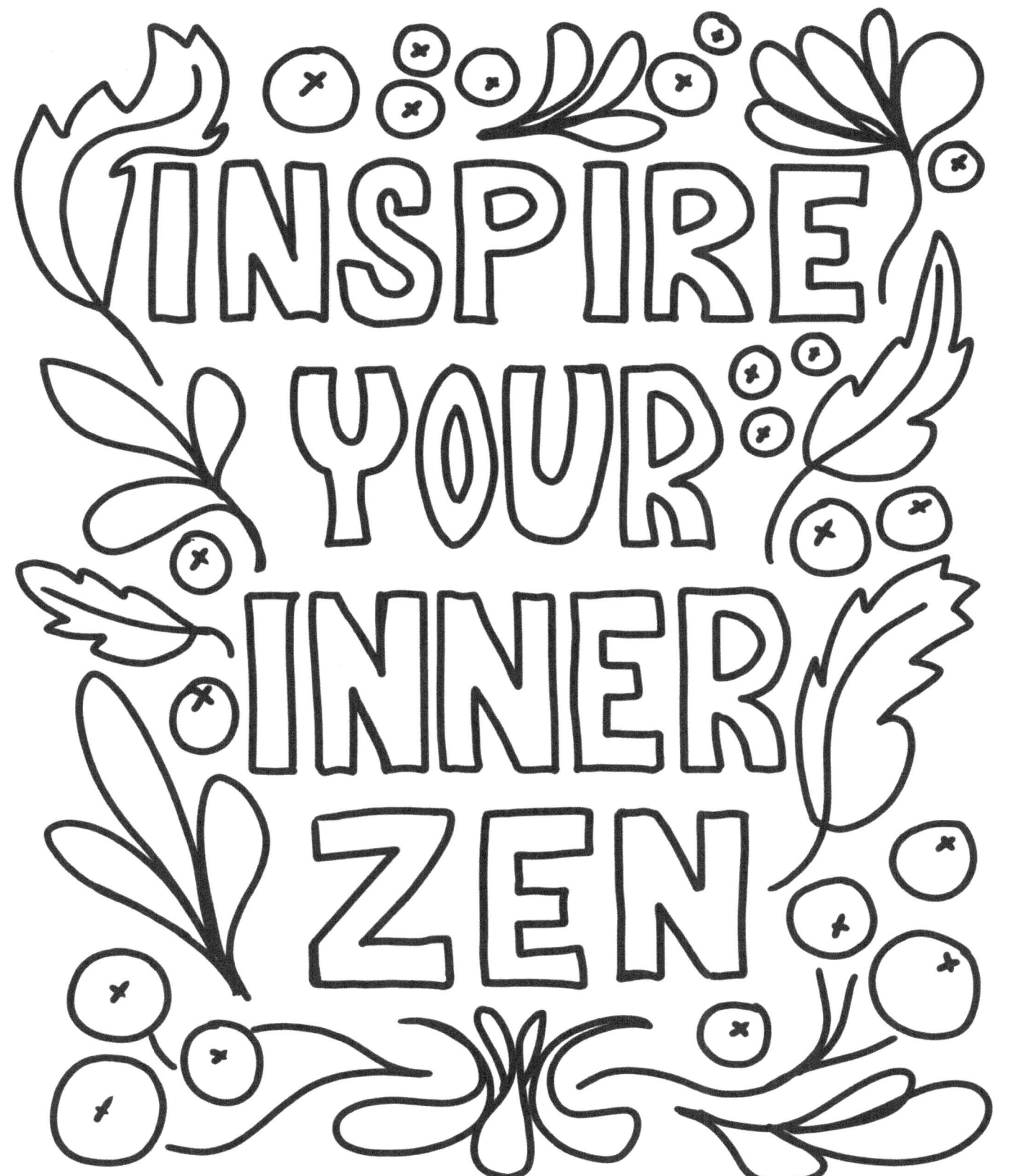

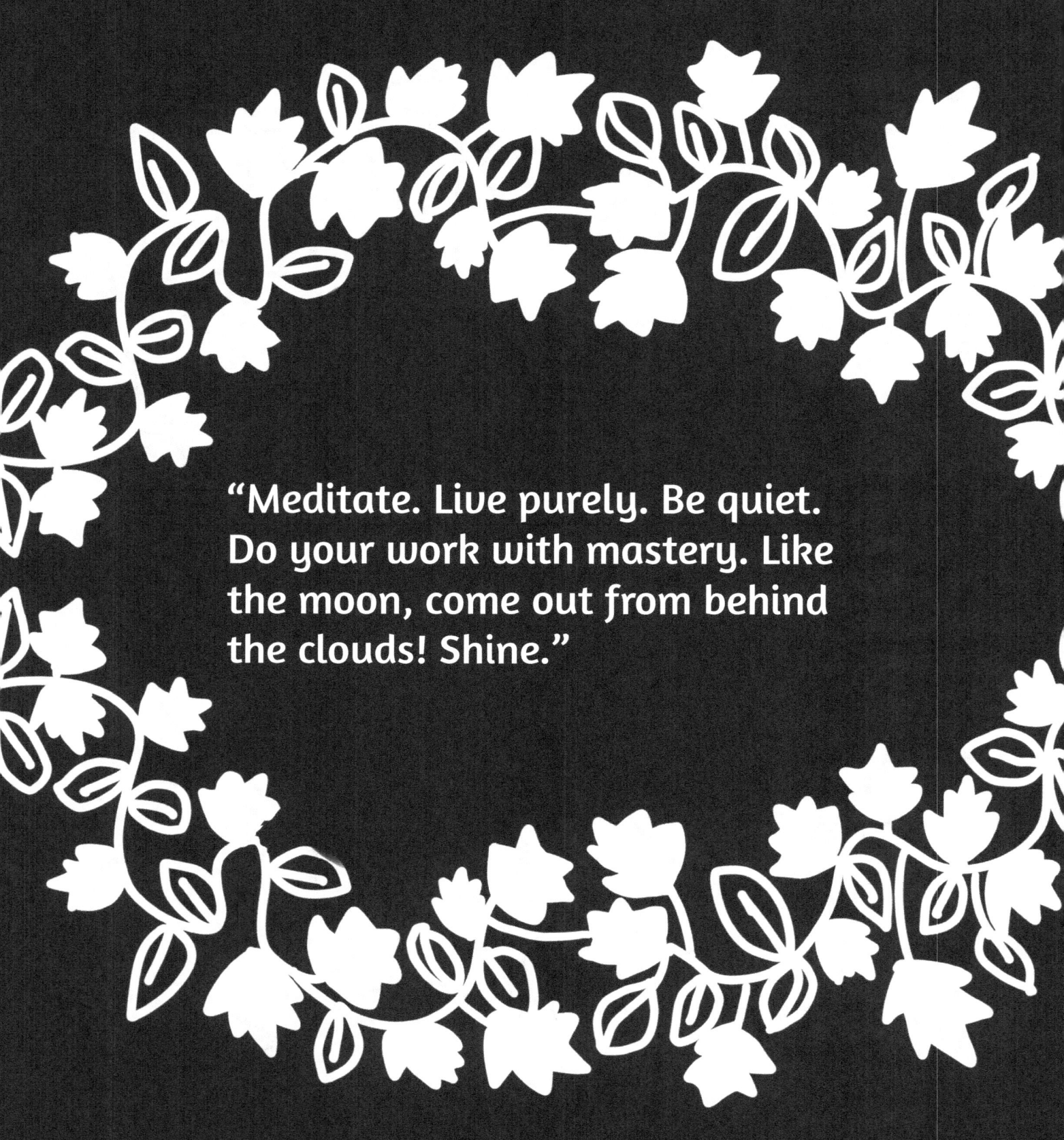

"Meditate. Live purely. Be quiet. Do your work with mastery. Like the moon, come out from behind the clouds! Shine."

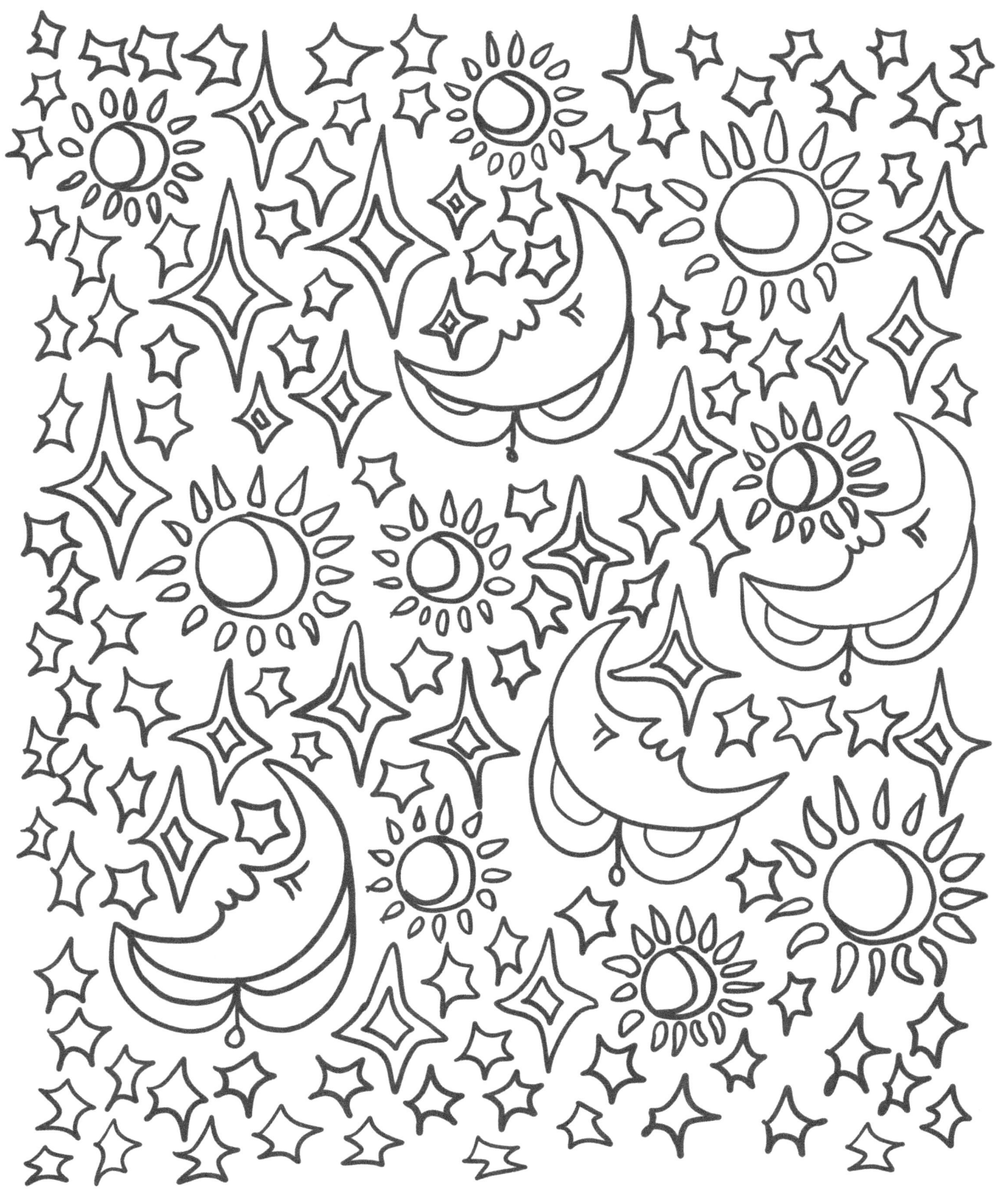

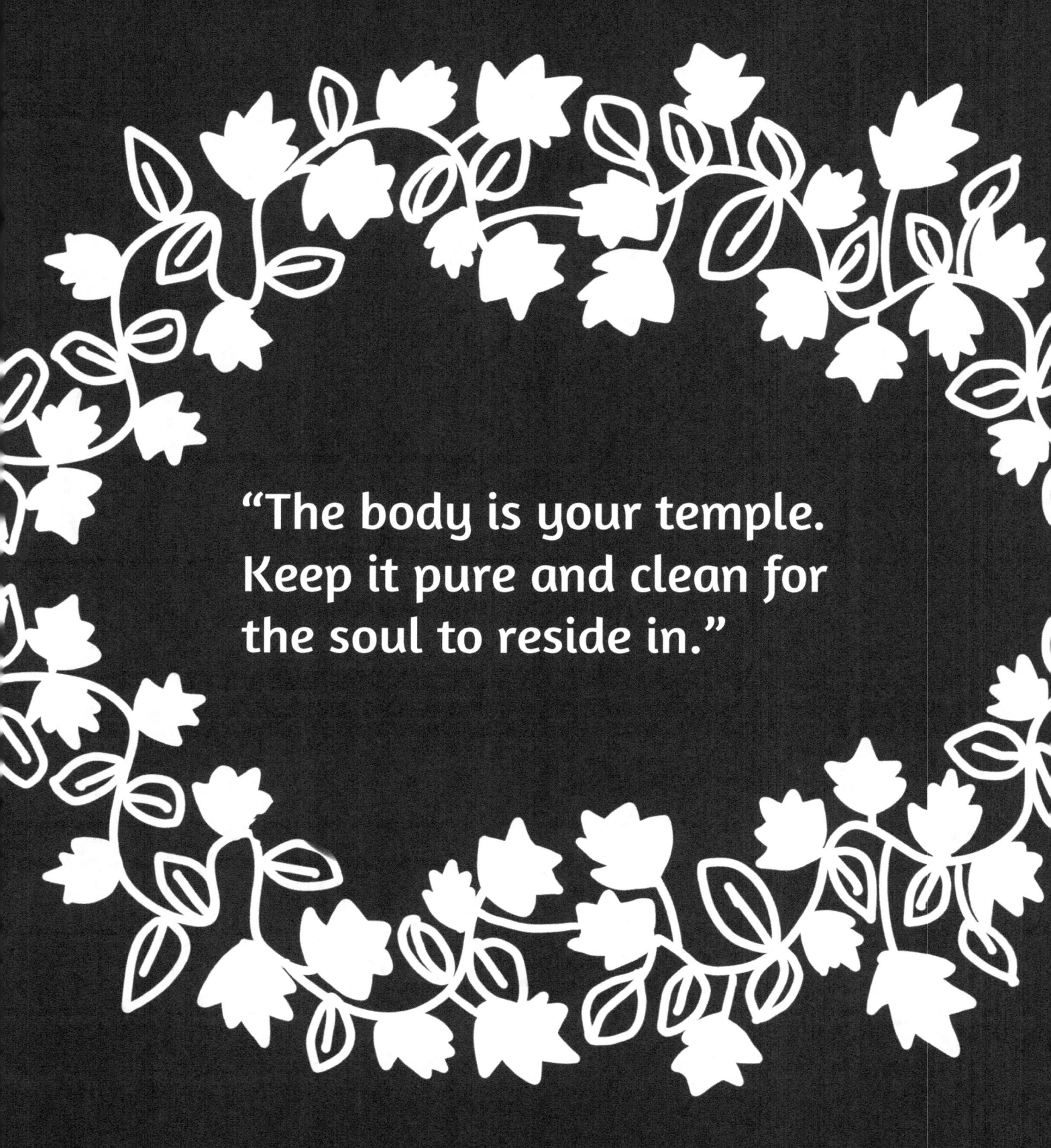

"The body is your temple. Keep it pure and clean for the soul to reside in."

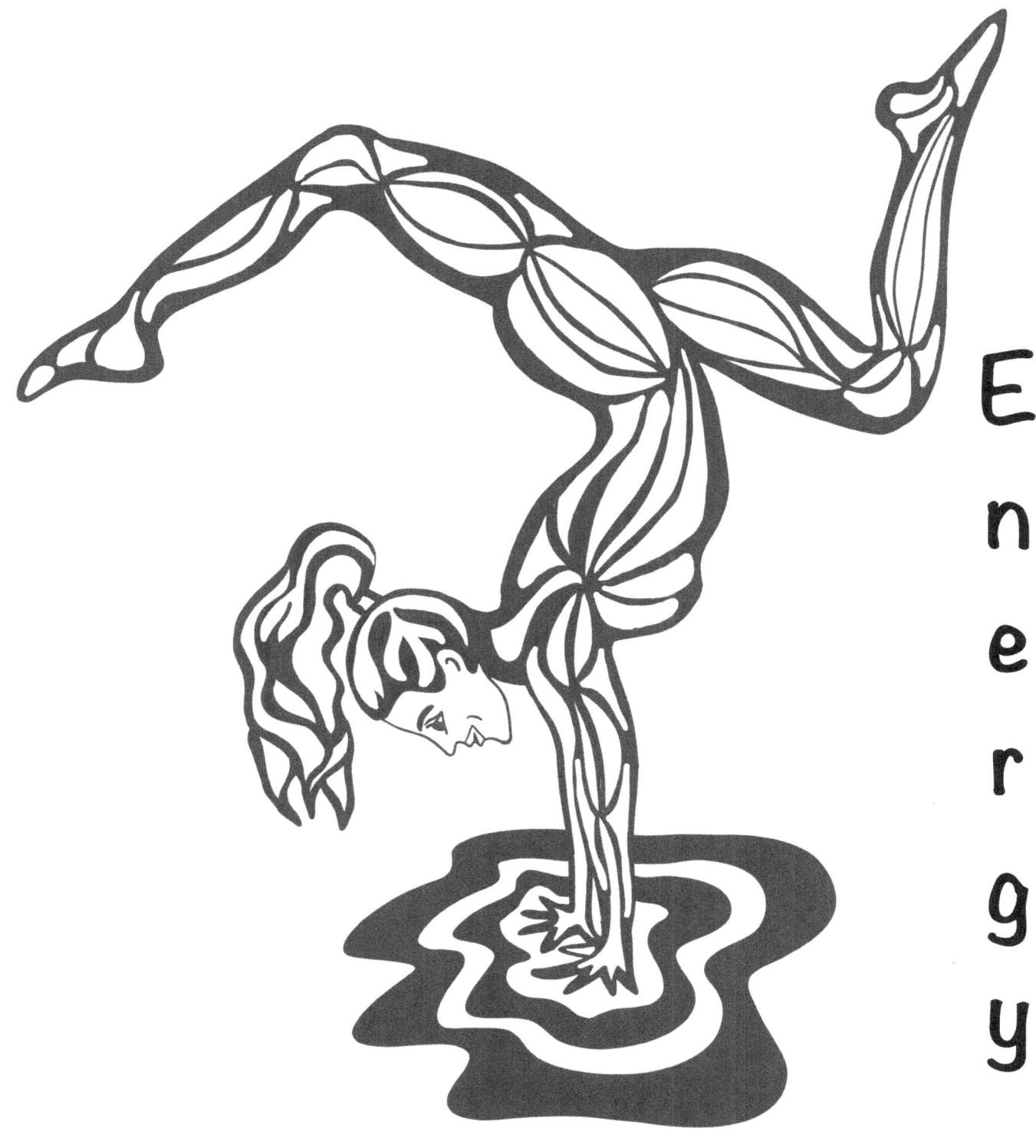

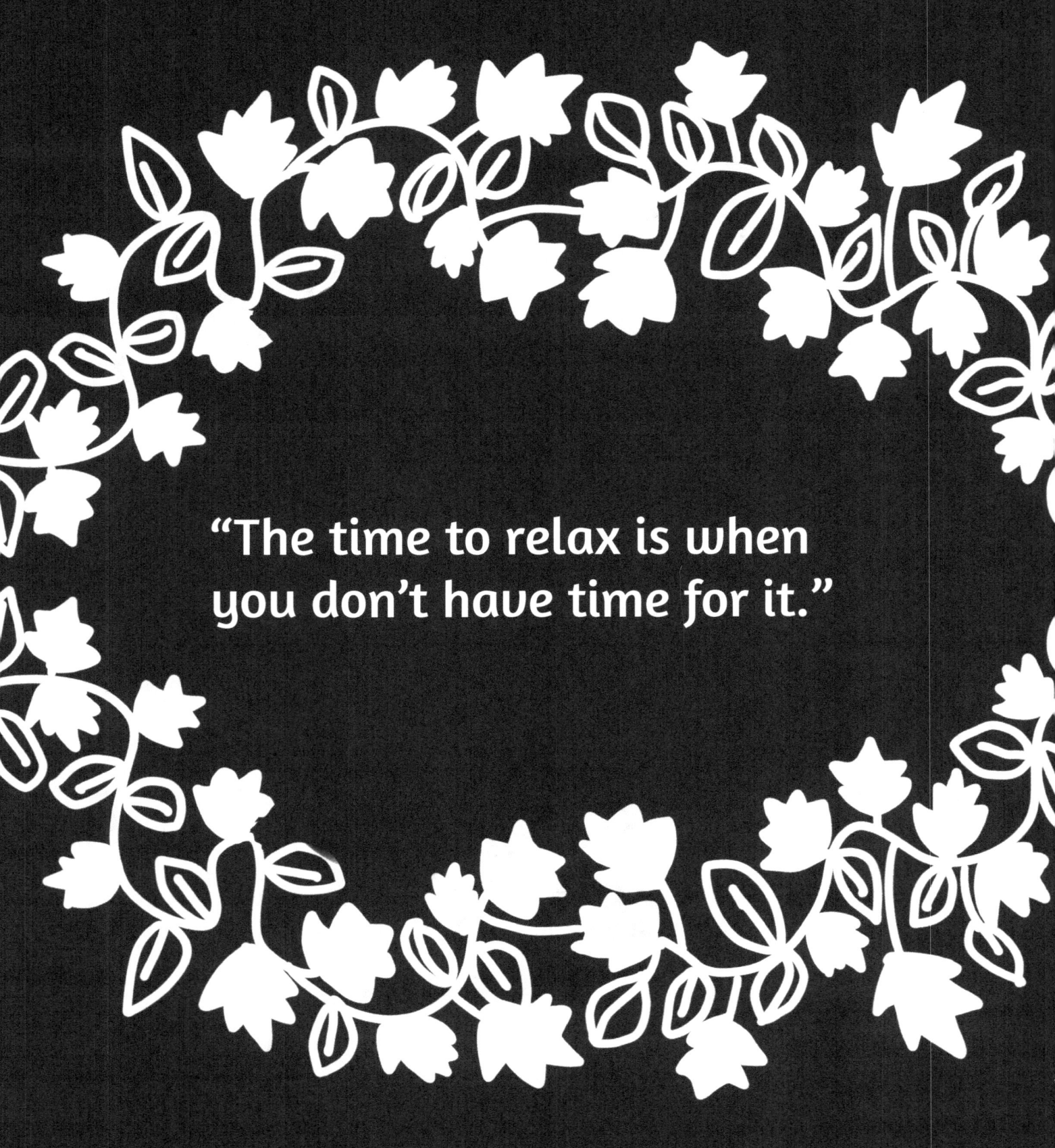

"The time to relax is when you don't have time for it."

Relax

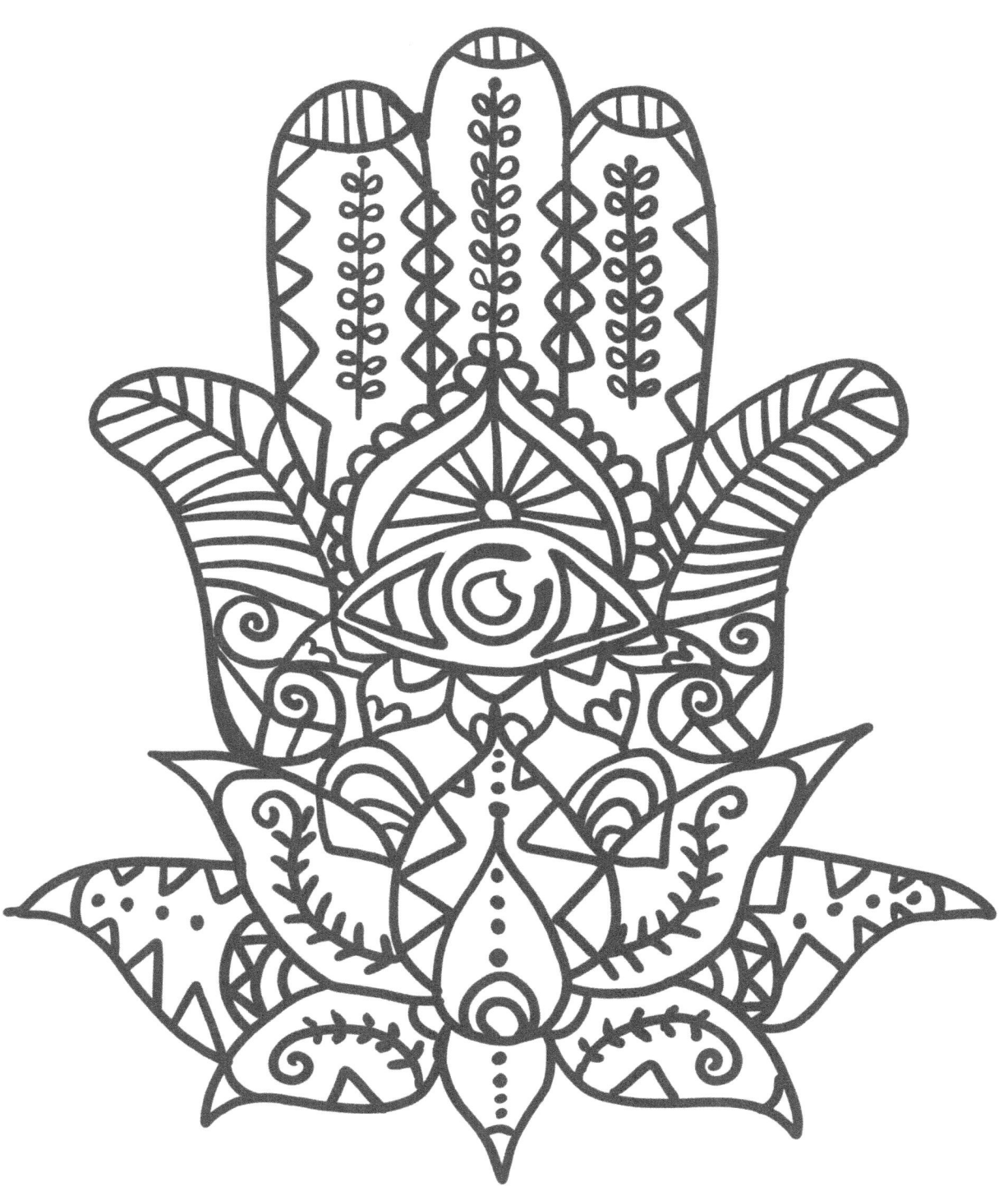

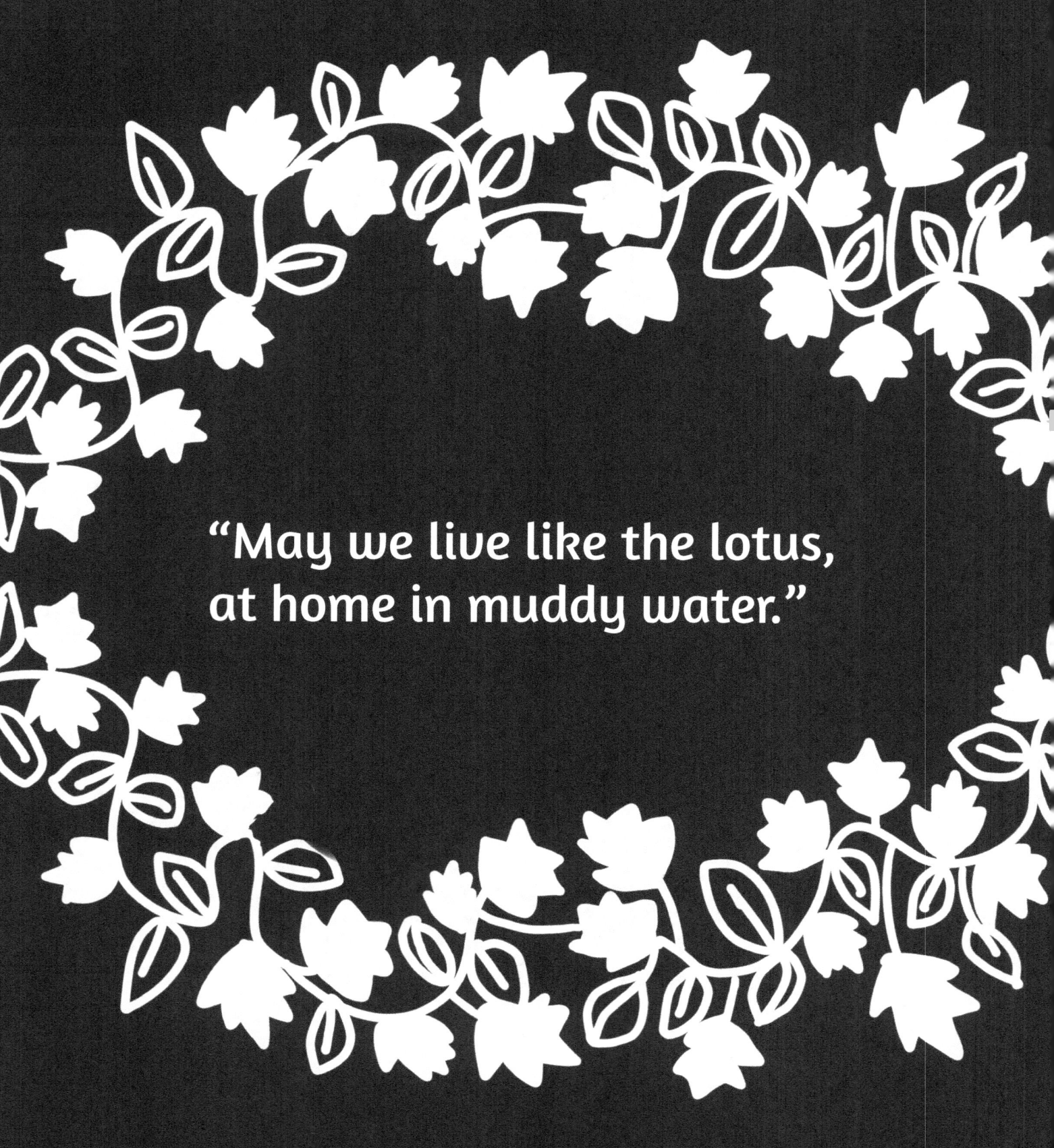

"May we live like the lotus, at home in muddy water."

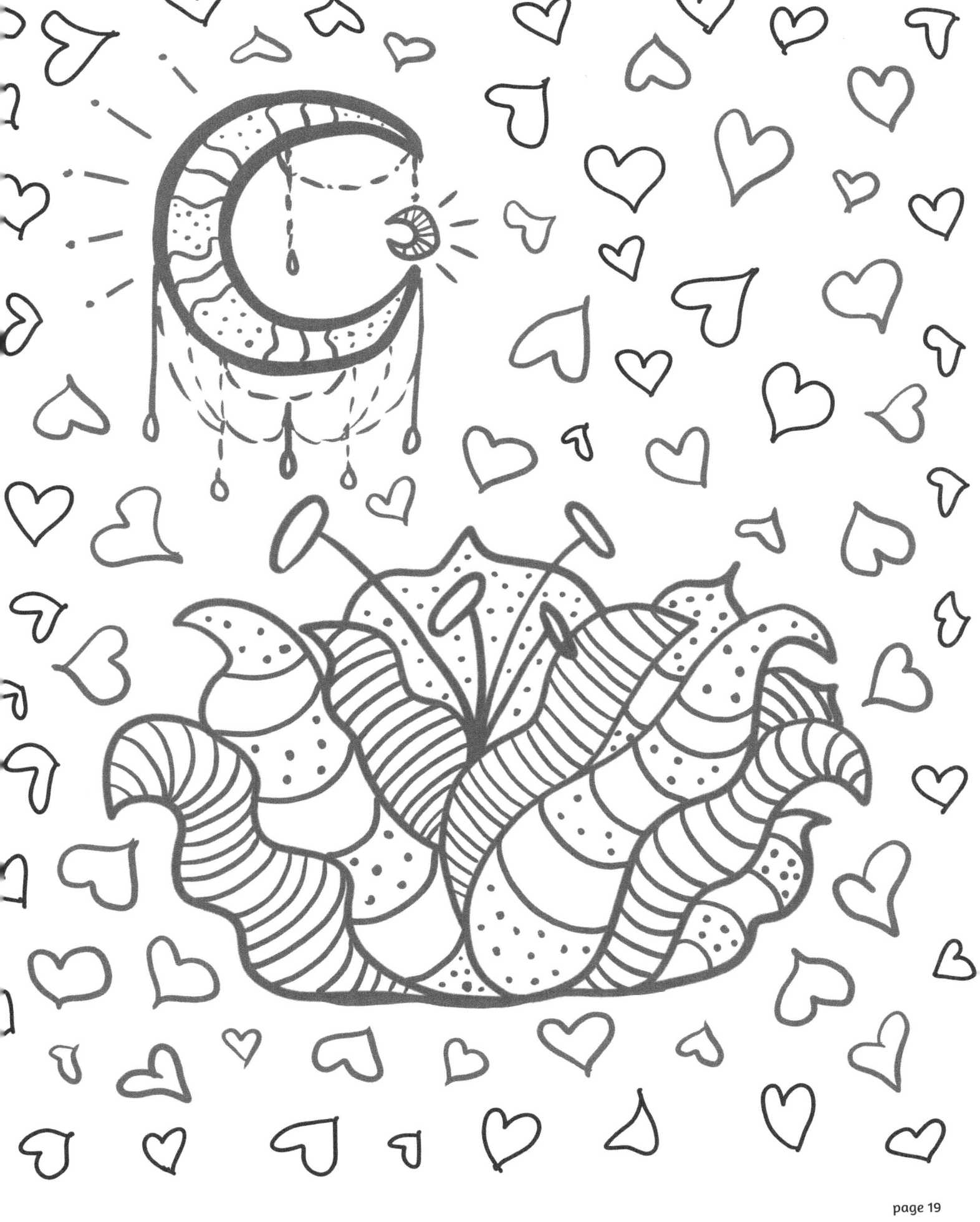

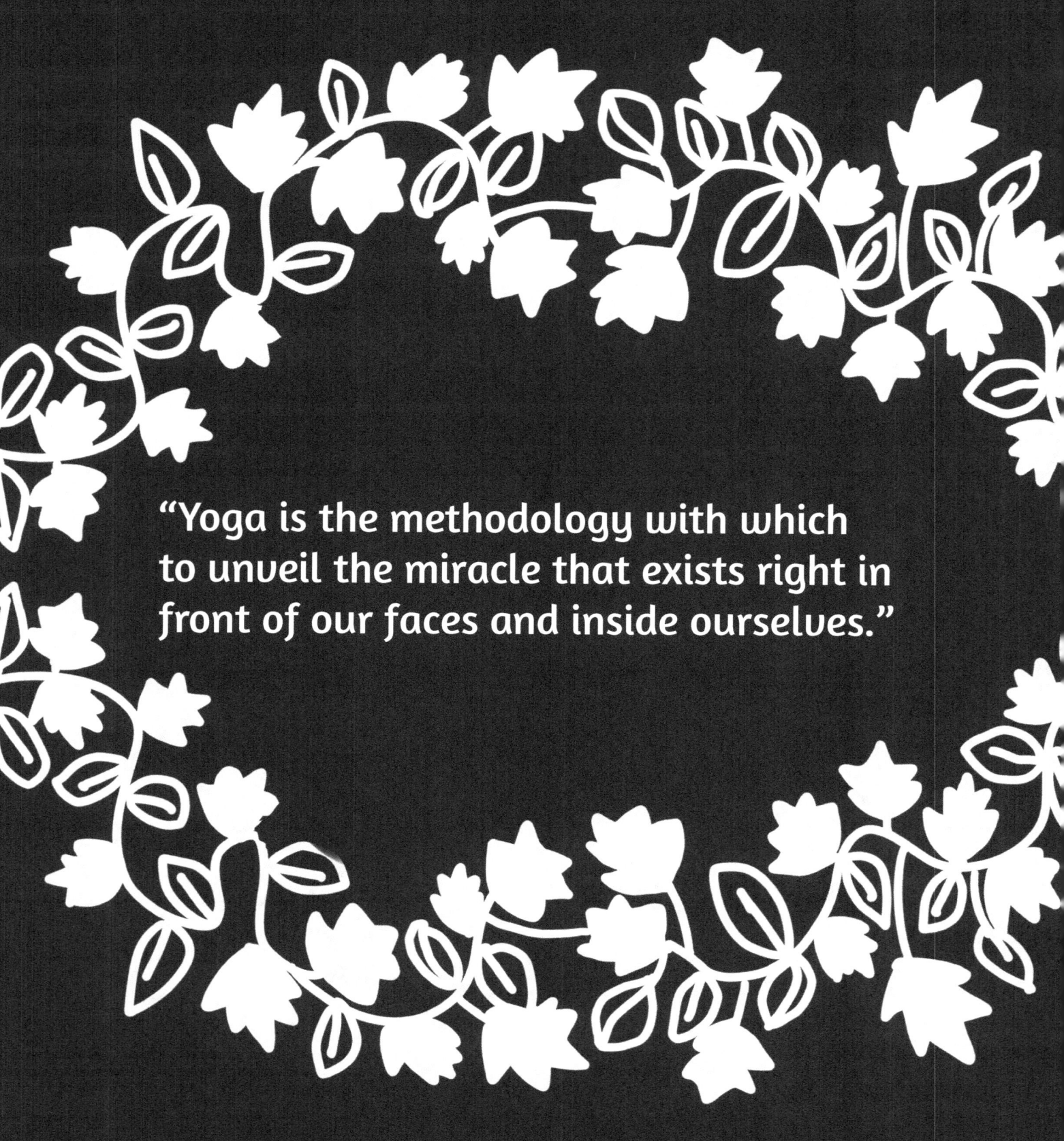

"Yoga is the methodology with which to unveil the miracle that exists right in front of our faces and inside ourselves."

Om Shanti

ॐ शान्तिः

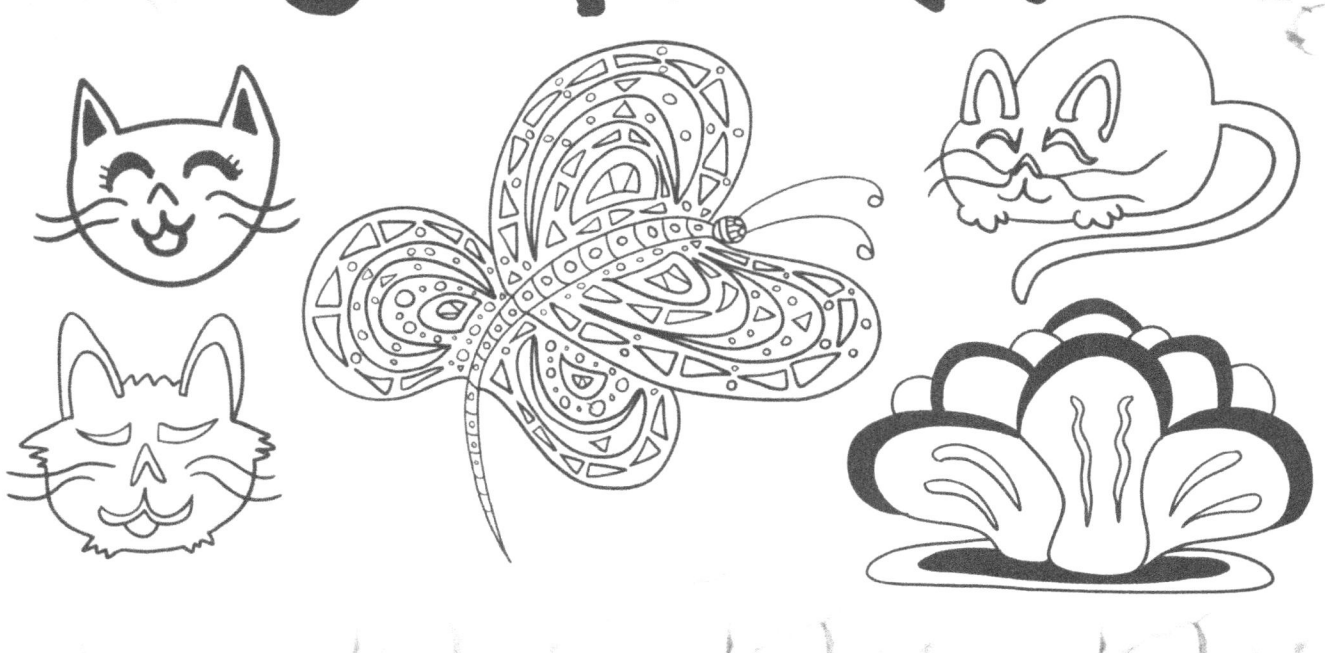

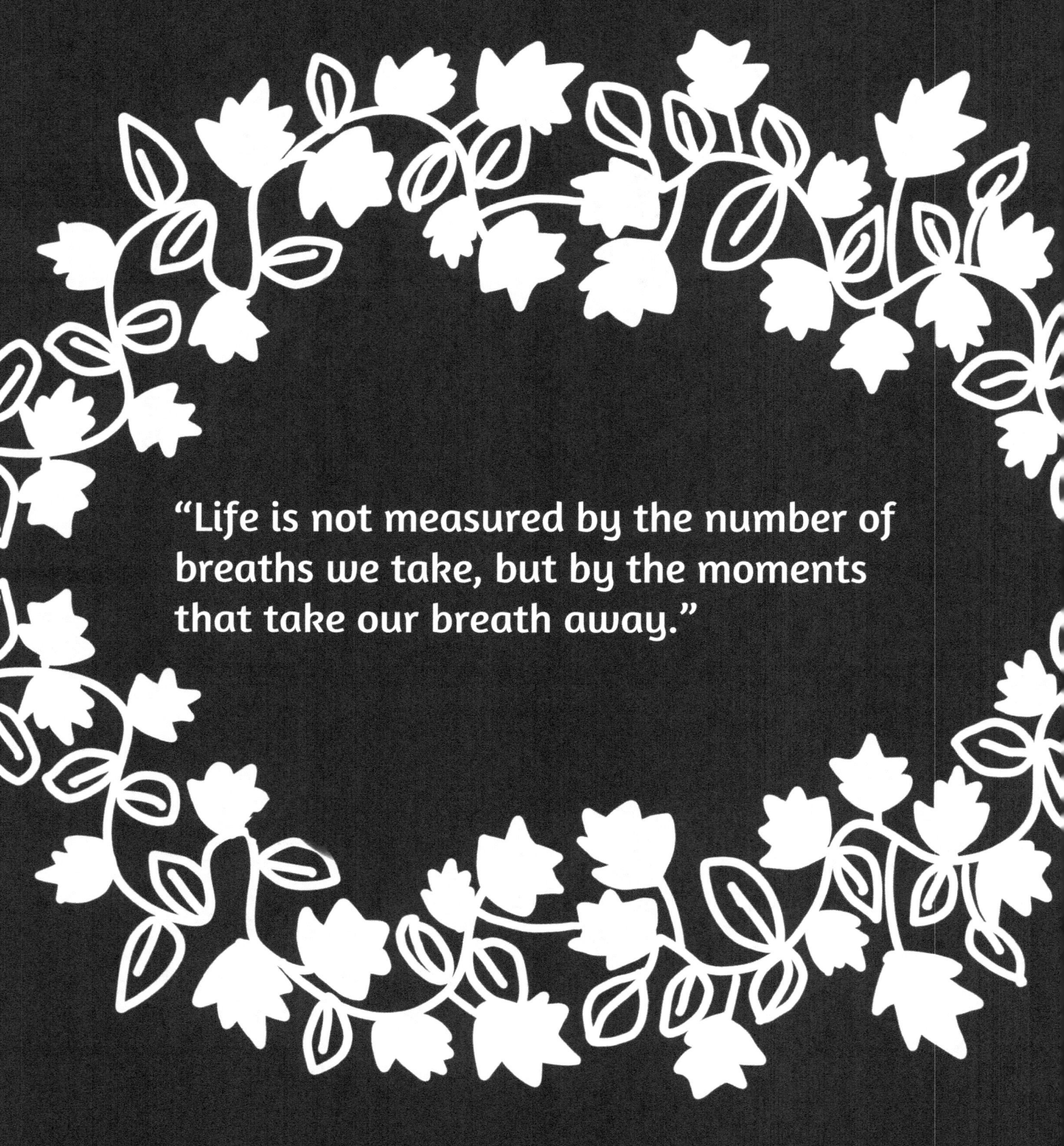

"Life is not measured by the number of breaths we take, but by the moments that take our breath away."

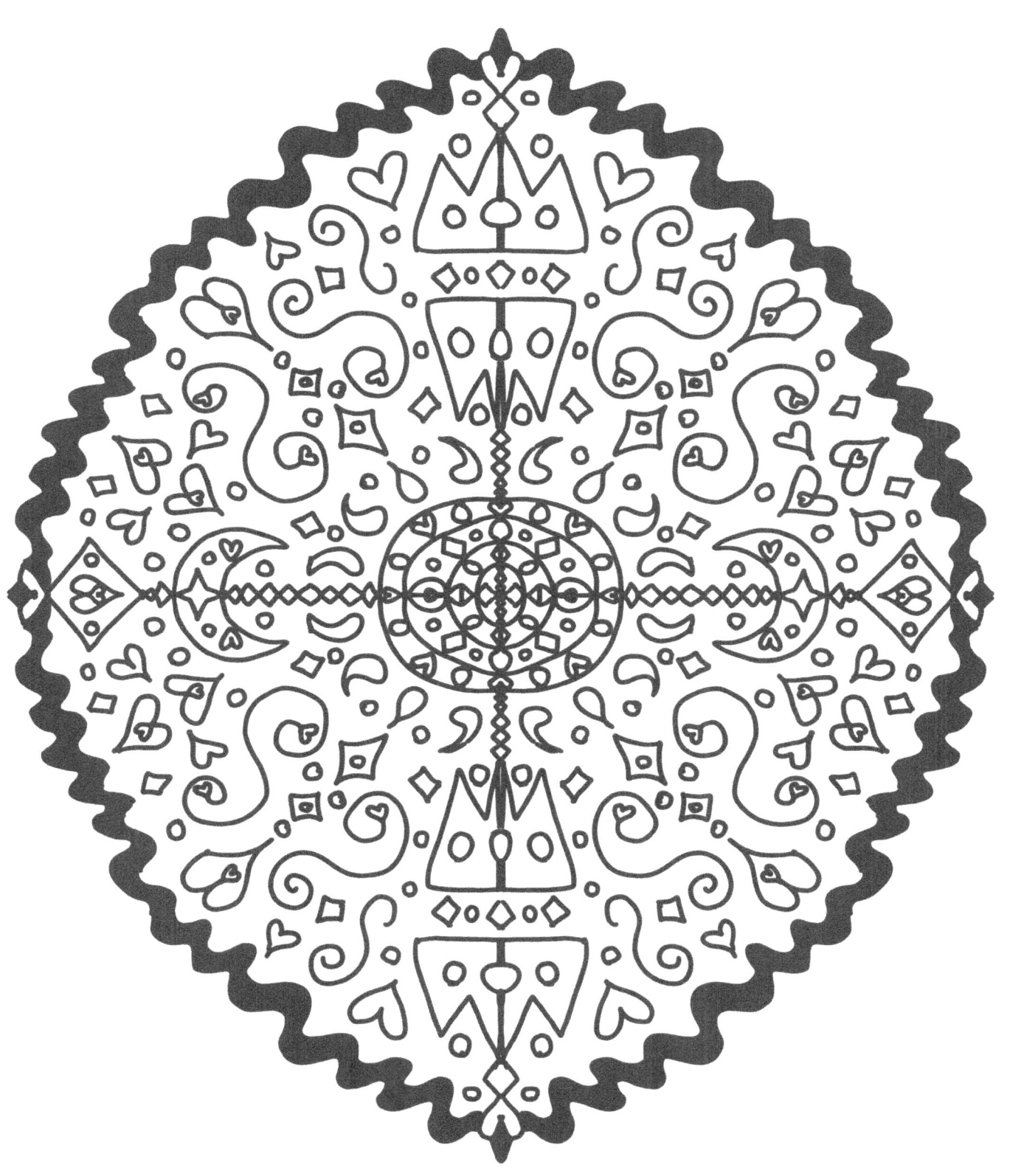

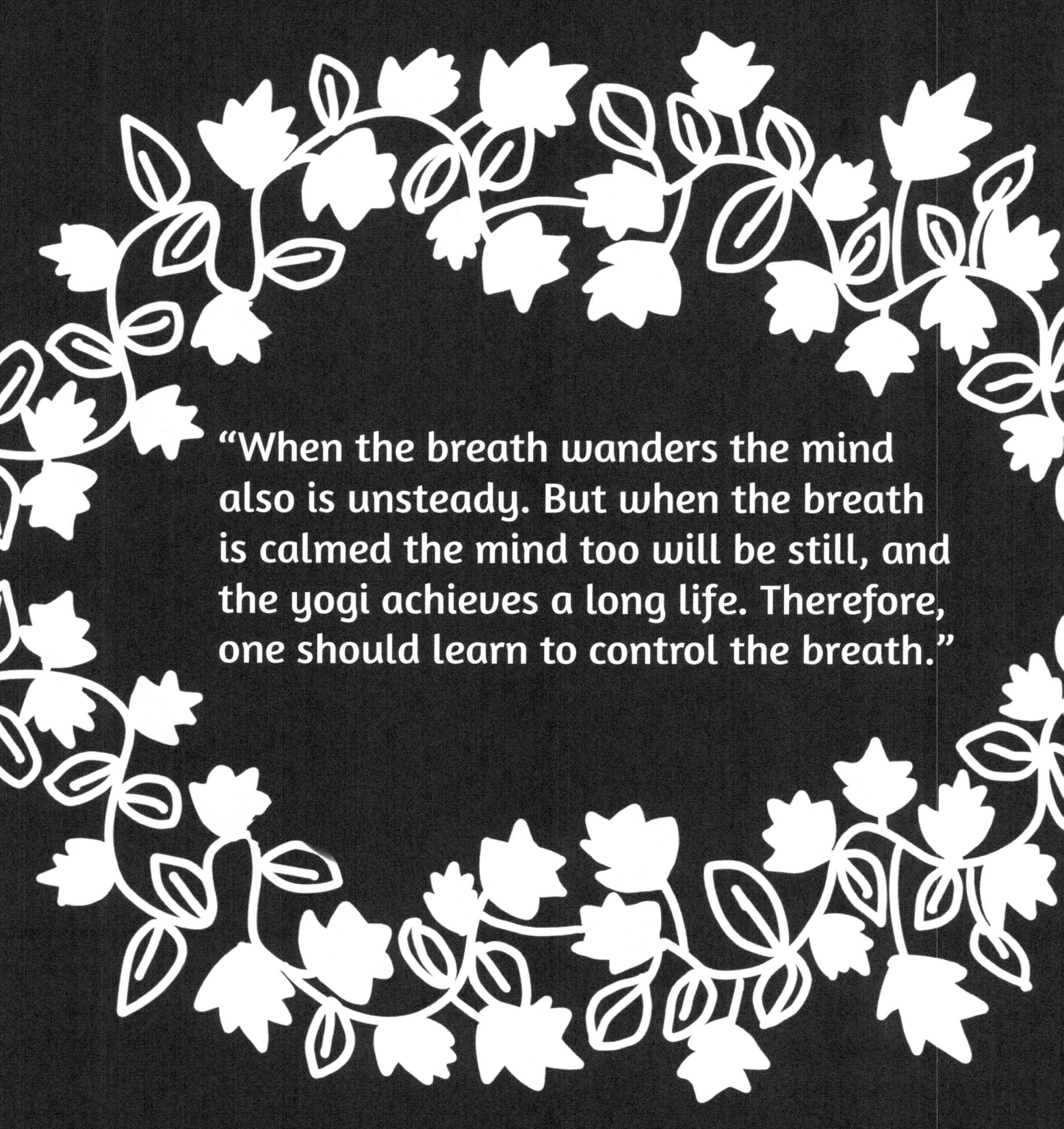

"When the breath wanders the mind also is unsteady. But when the breath is calmed the mind too will be still, and the yogi achieves a long life. Therefore, one should learn to control the breath."

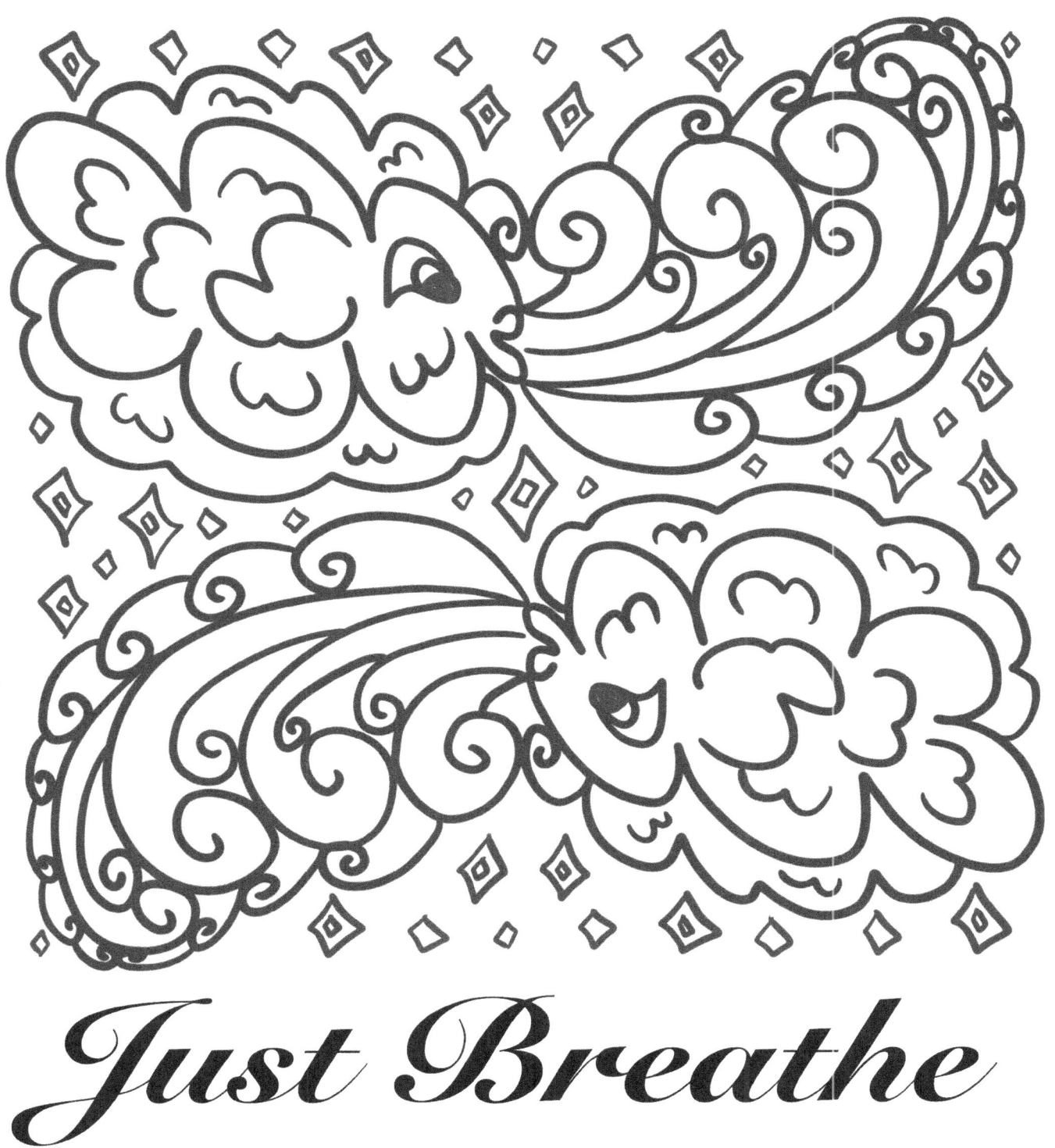

Just Breathe

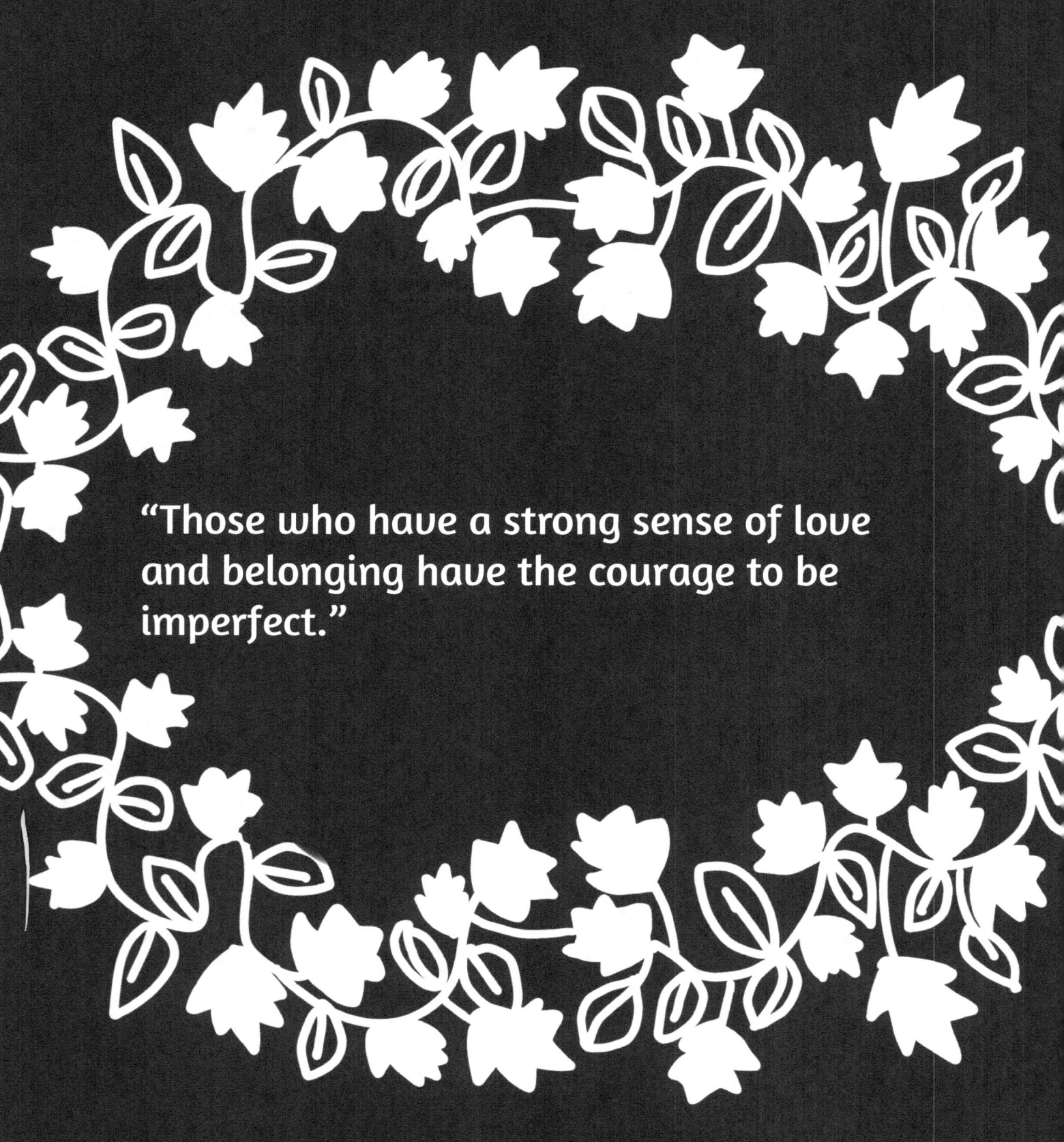

"Those who have a strong sense of love and belonging have the courage to be imperfect."

Third-eye

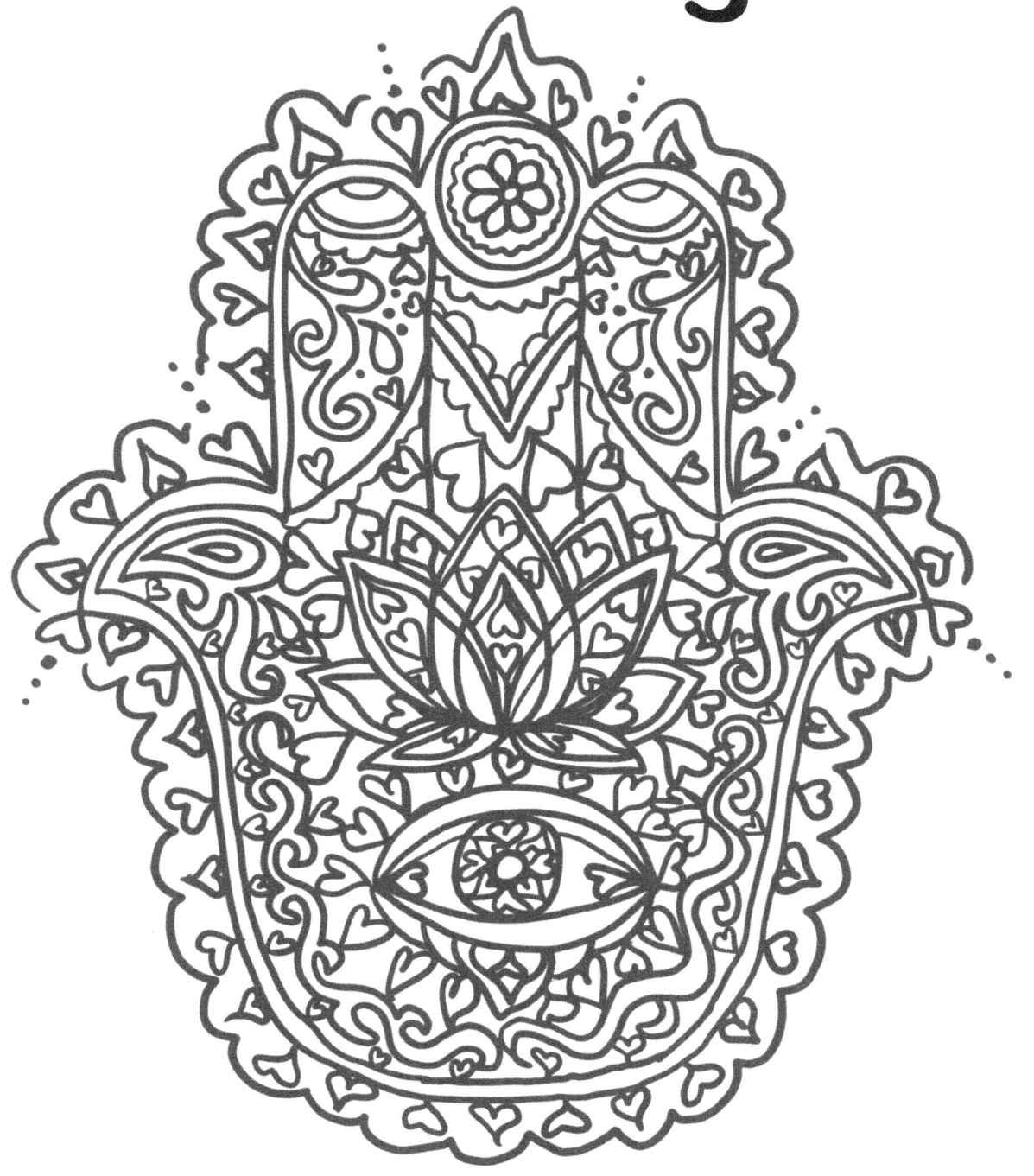

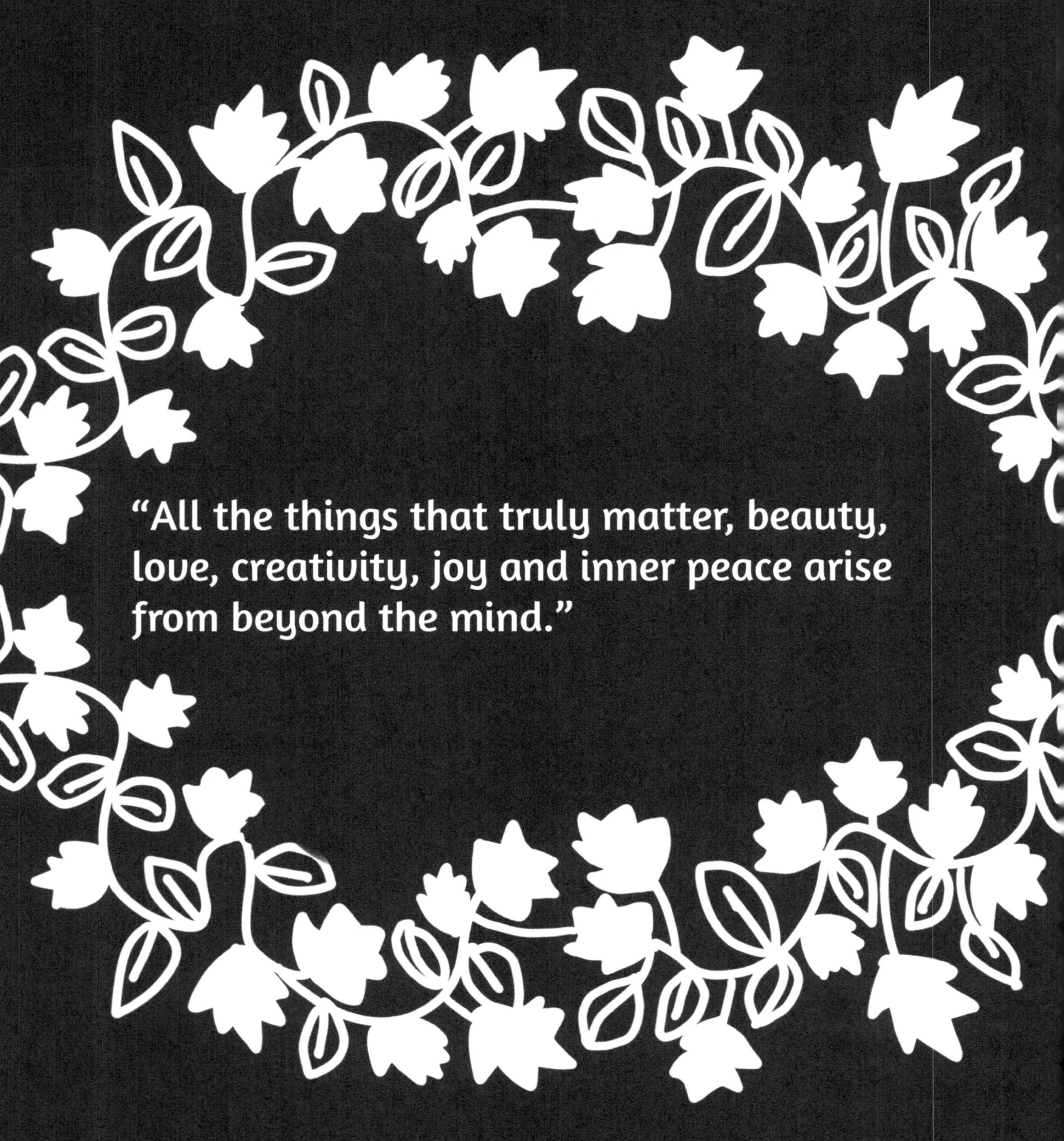

"All the things that truly matter, beauty, love, creativity, joy and inner peace arise from beyond the mind."

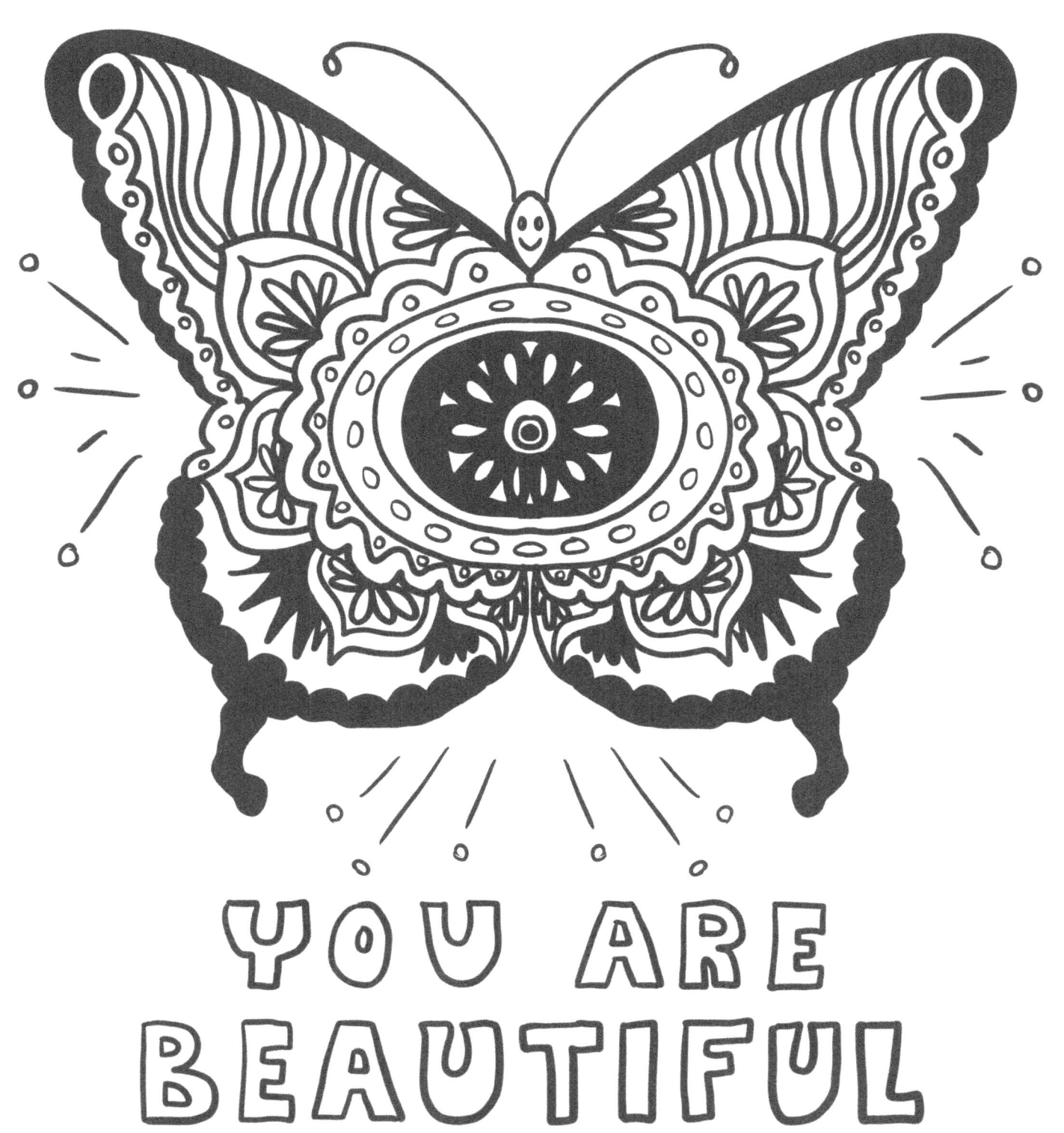

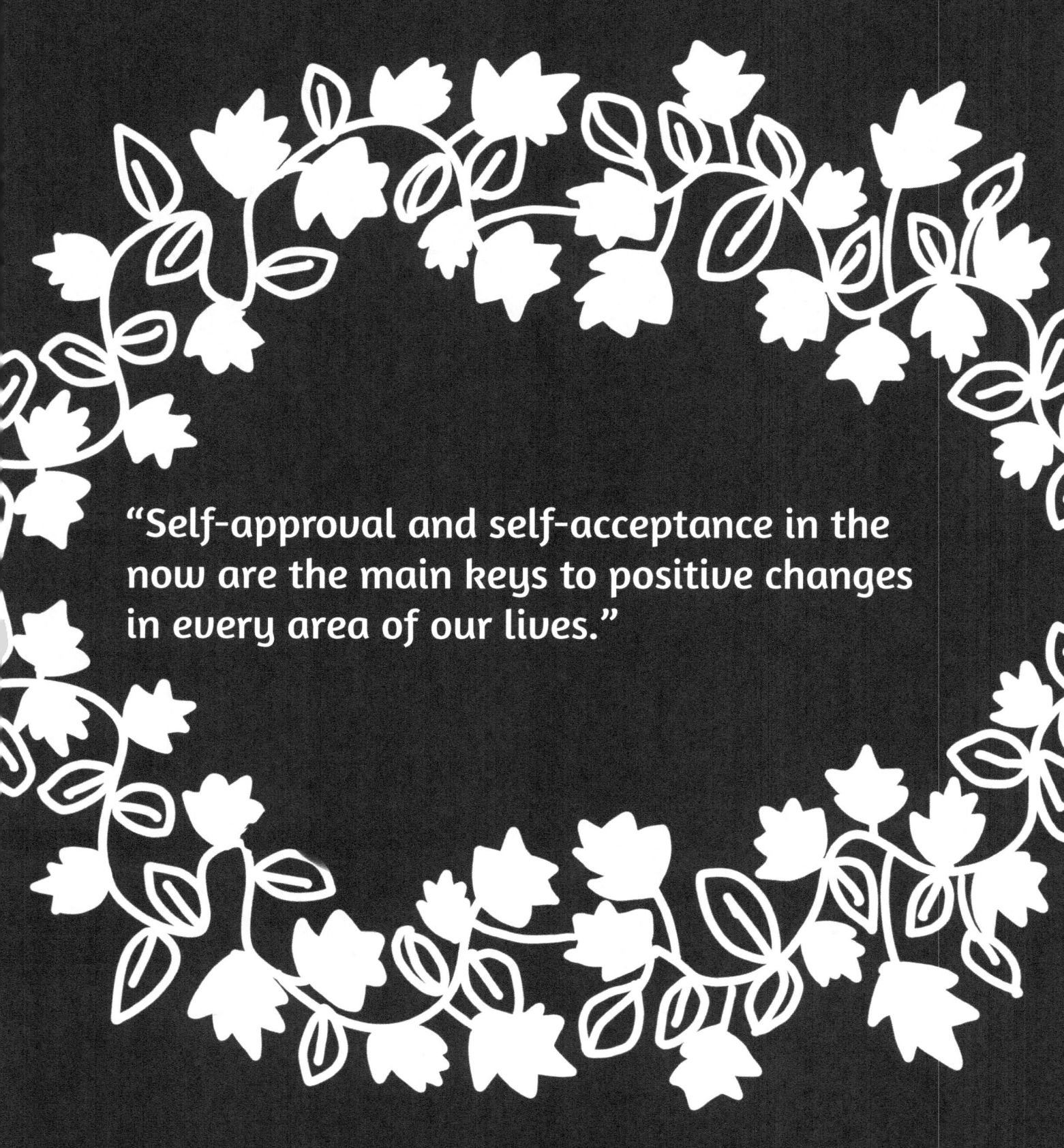

"Self-approval and self-acceptance in the now are the main keys to positive changes in every area of our lives."

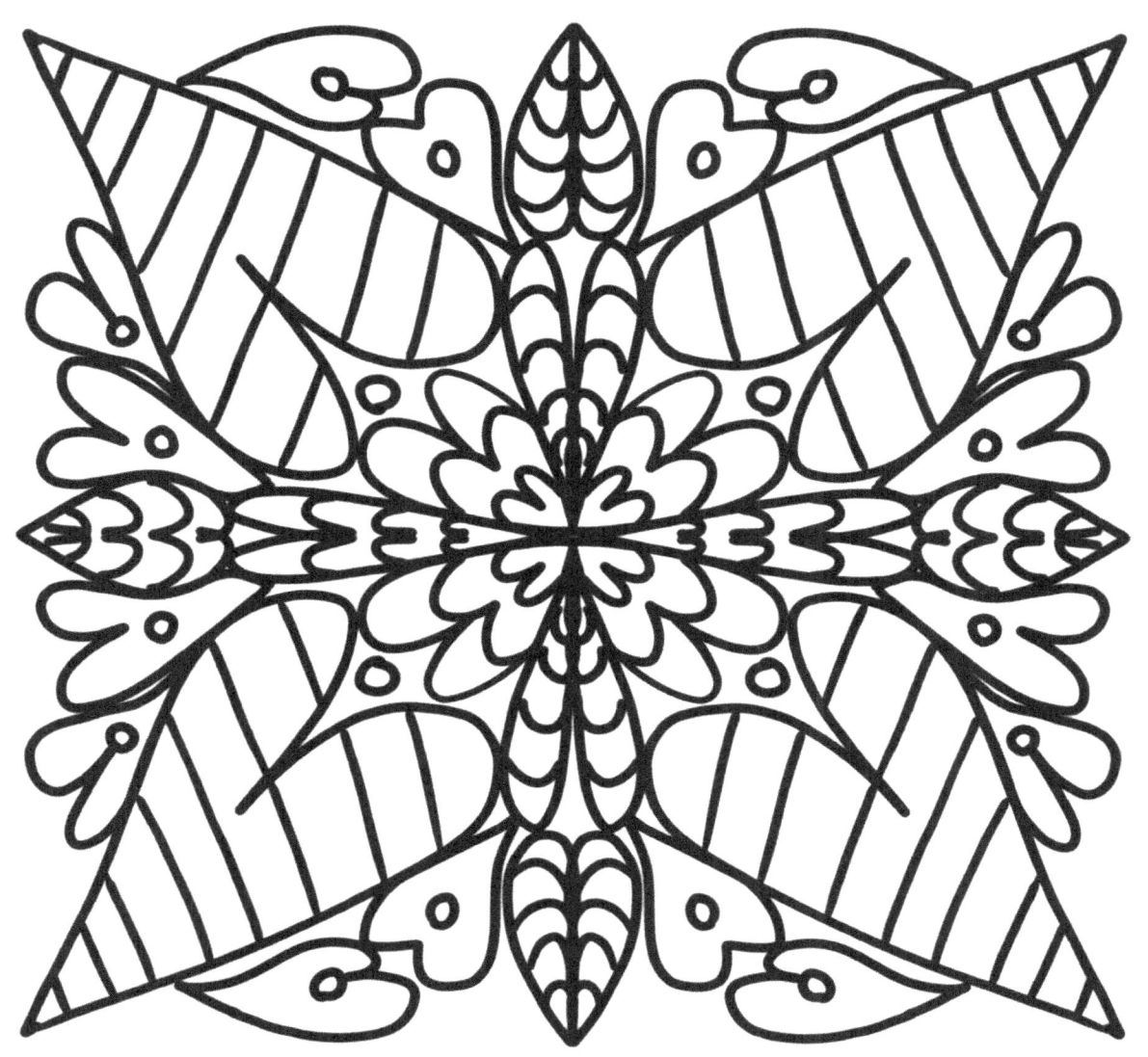

Life Force

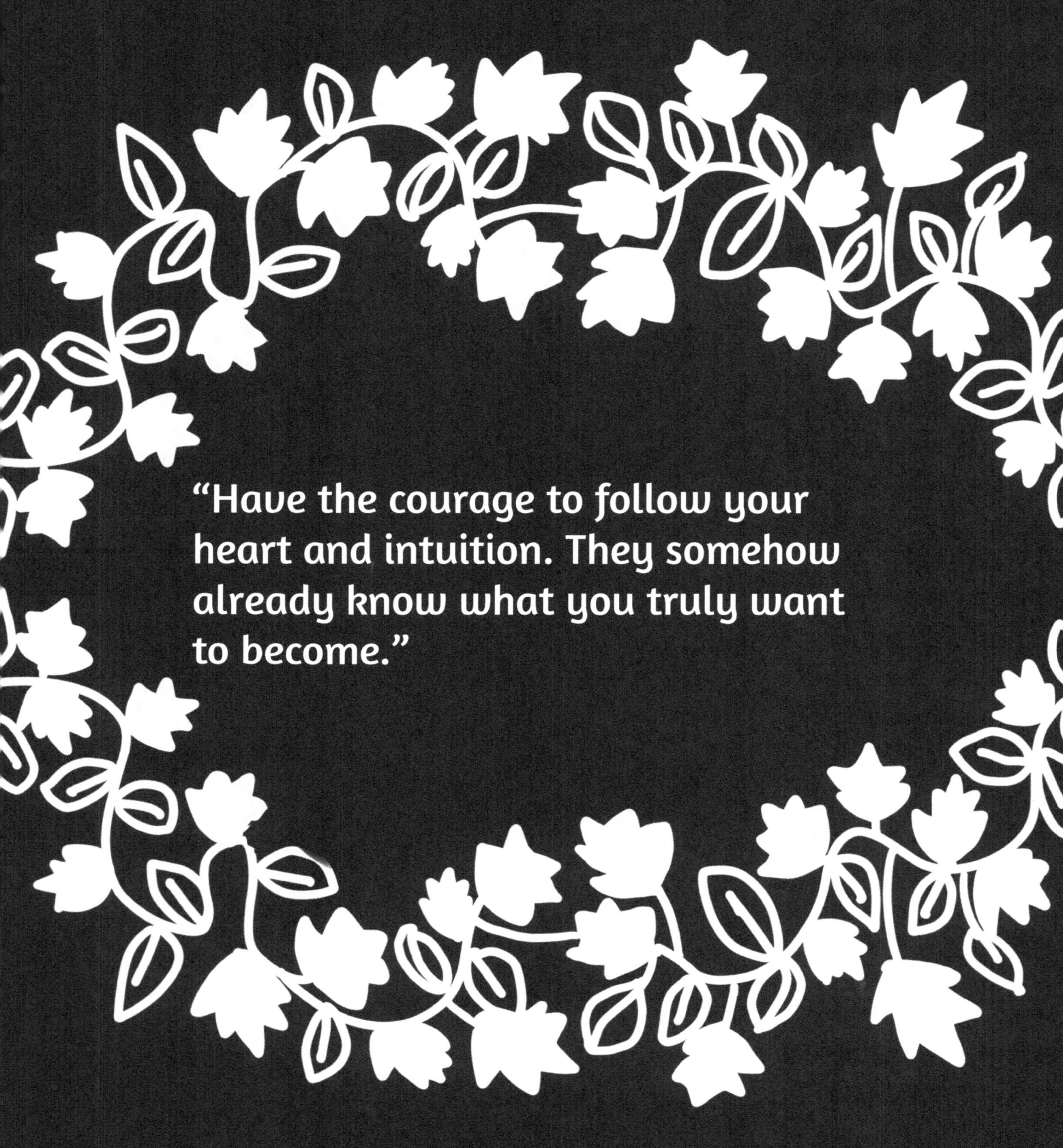

"Have the courage to follow your heart and intuition. They somehow already know what you truly want to become."

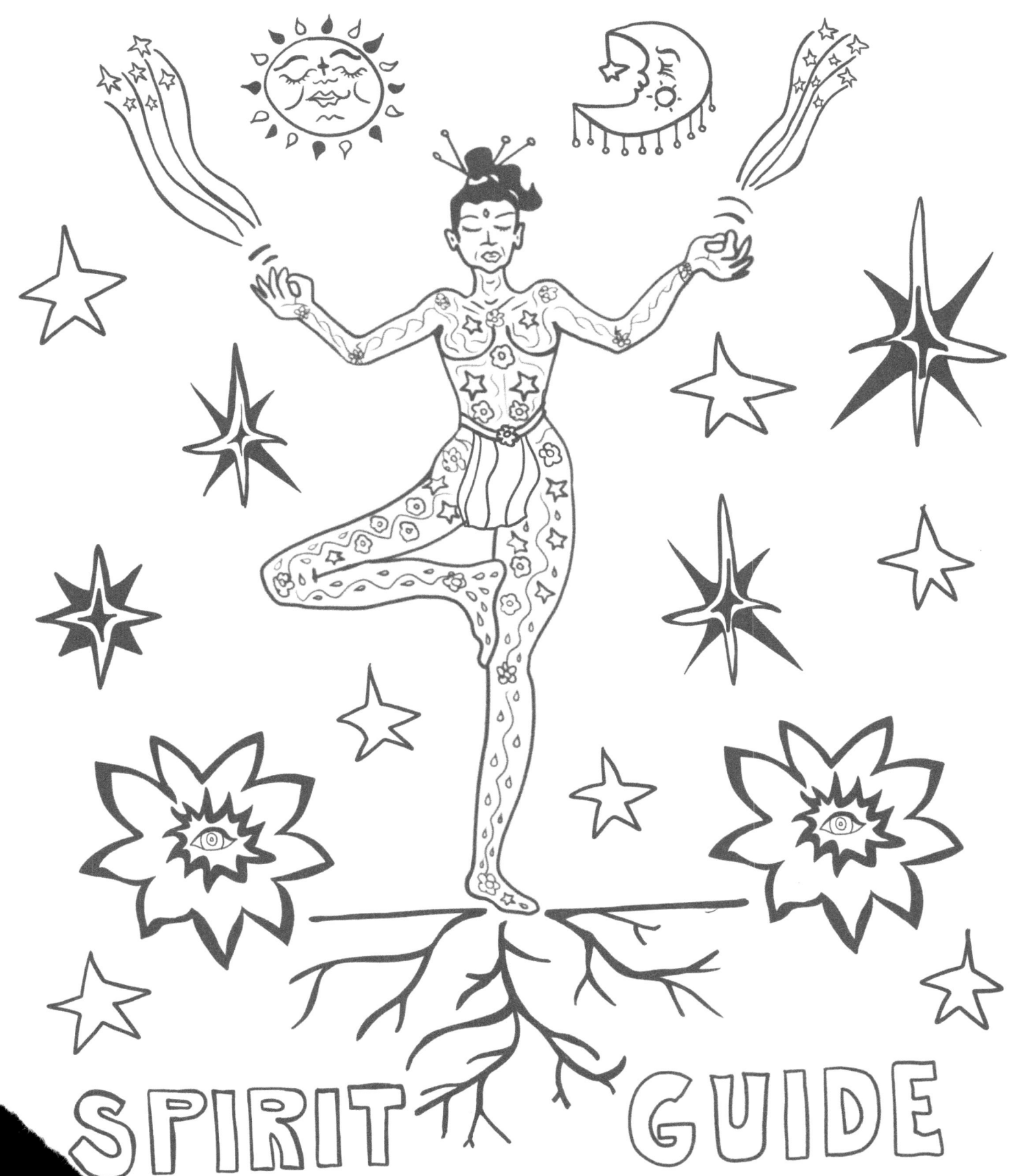

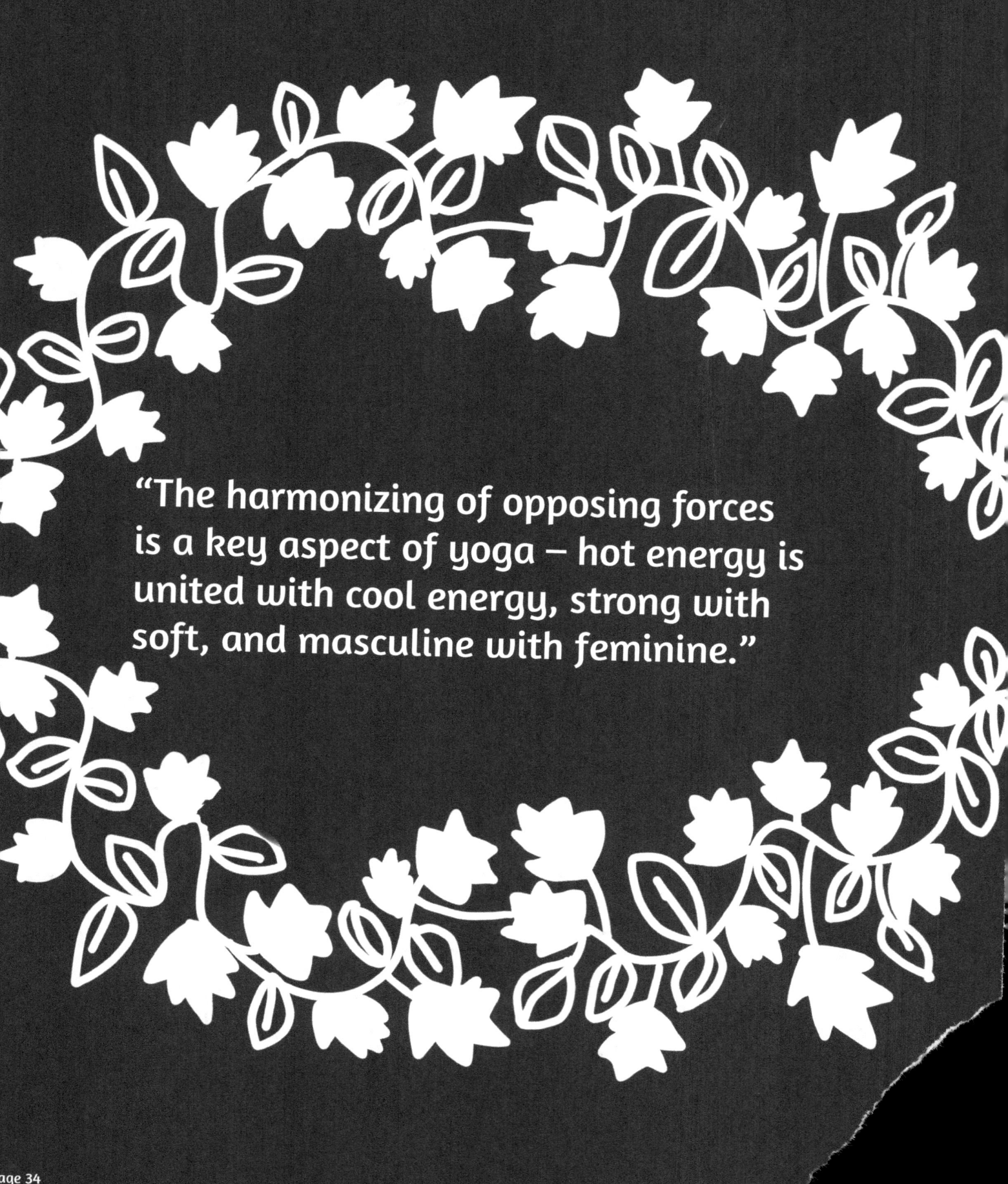

"The harmonizing of opposing forces is a key aspect of yoga – hot energy is united with cool energy, strong with soft, and masculine with feminine."

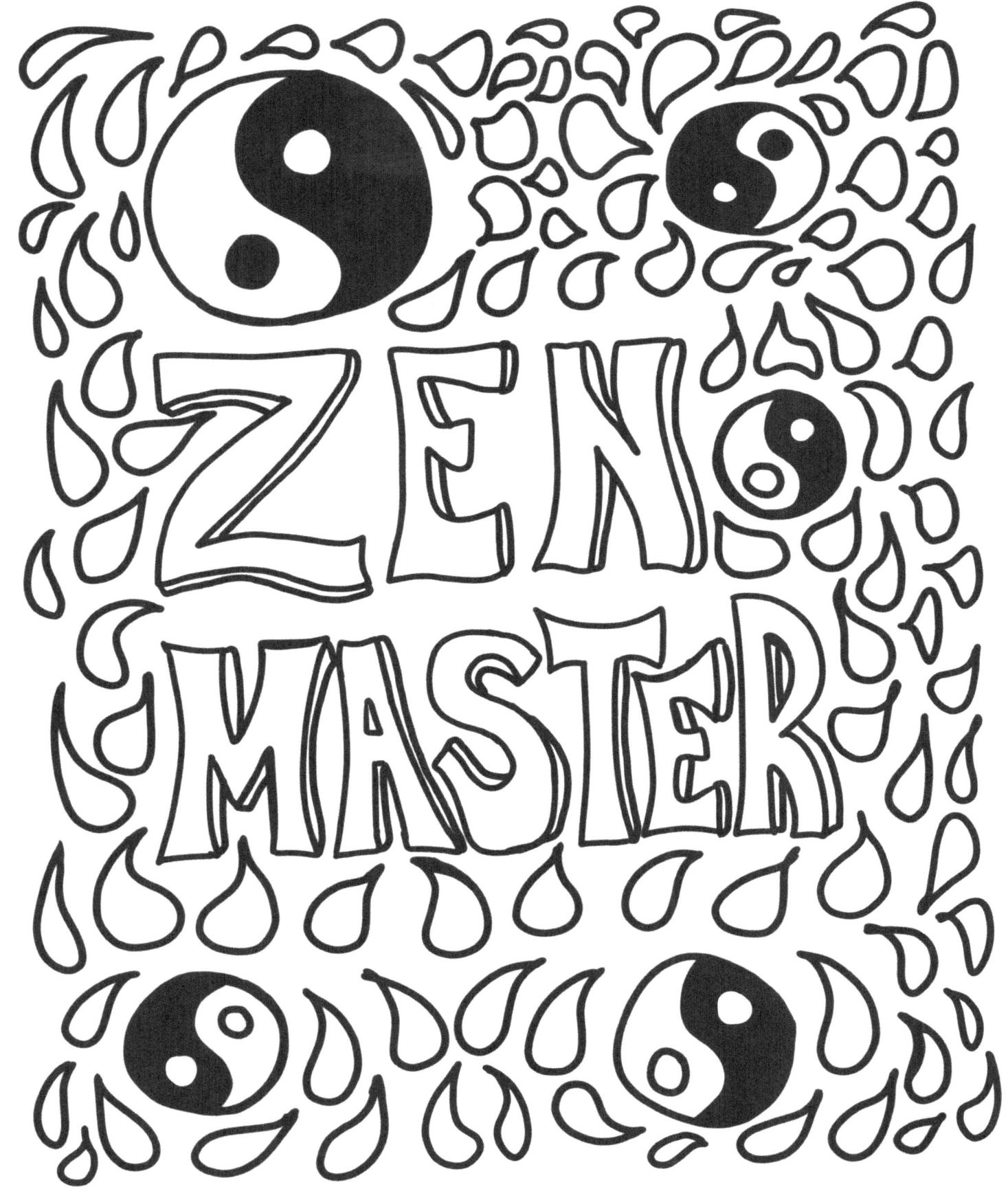

"You must be the change you wish to see in the world."

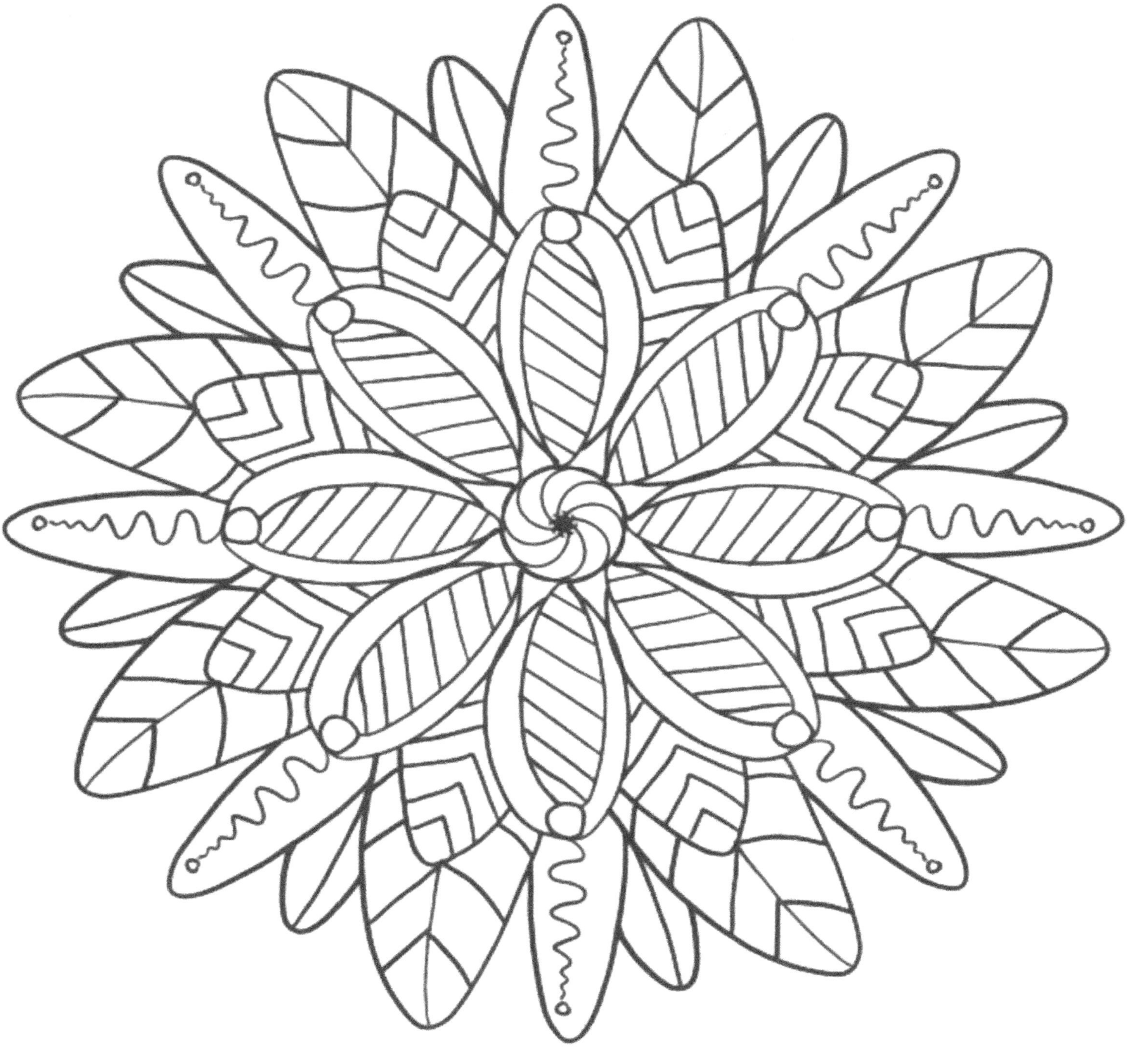

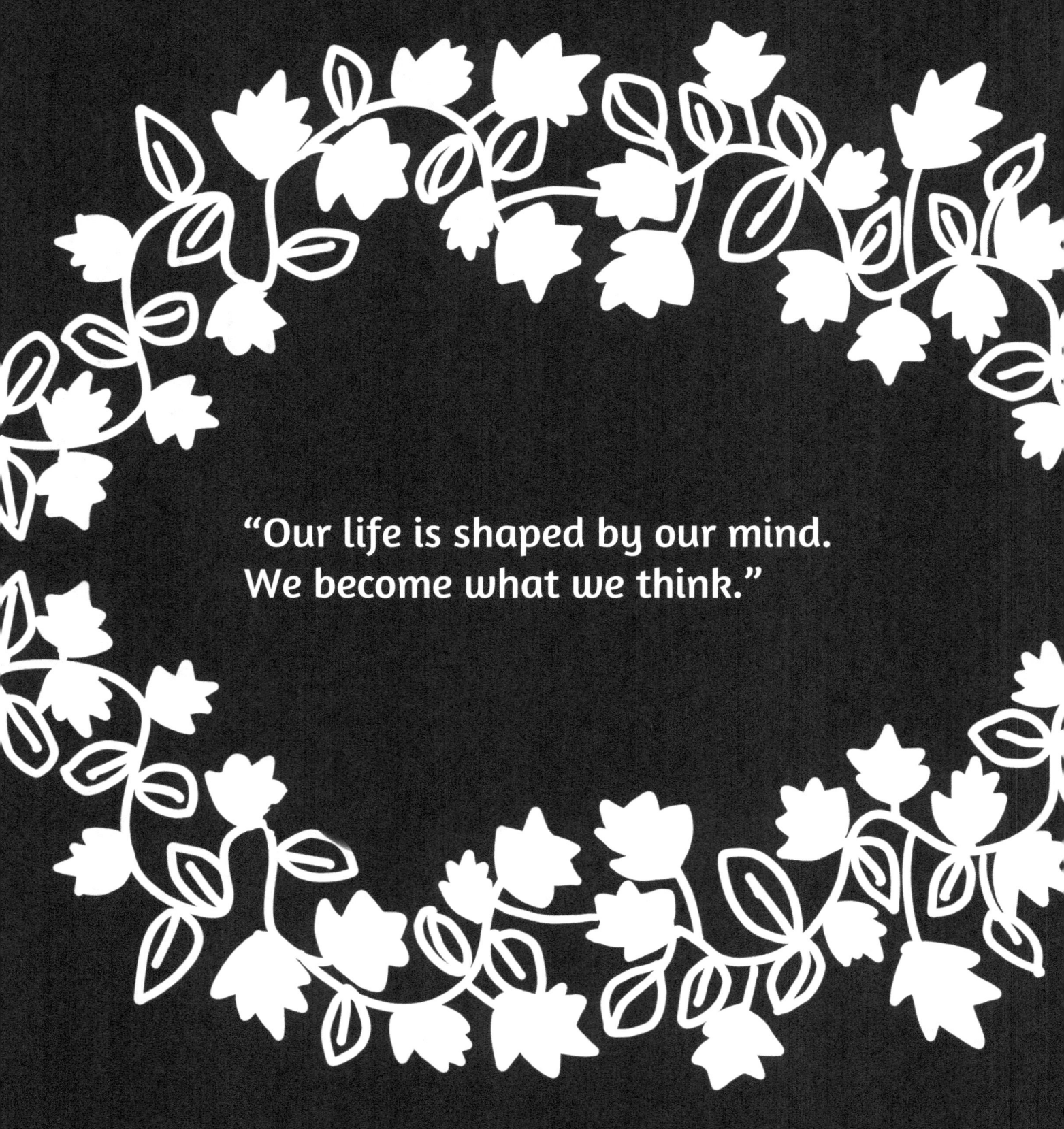
"Our life is shaped by our mind. We become what we think."

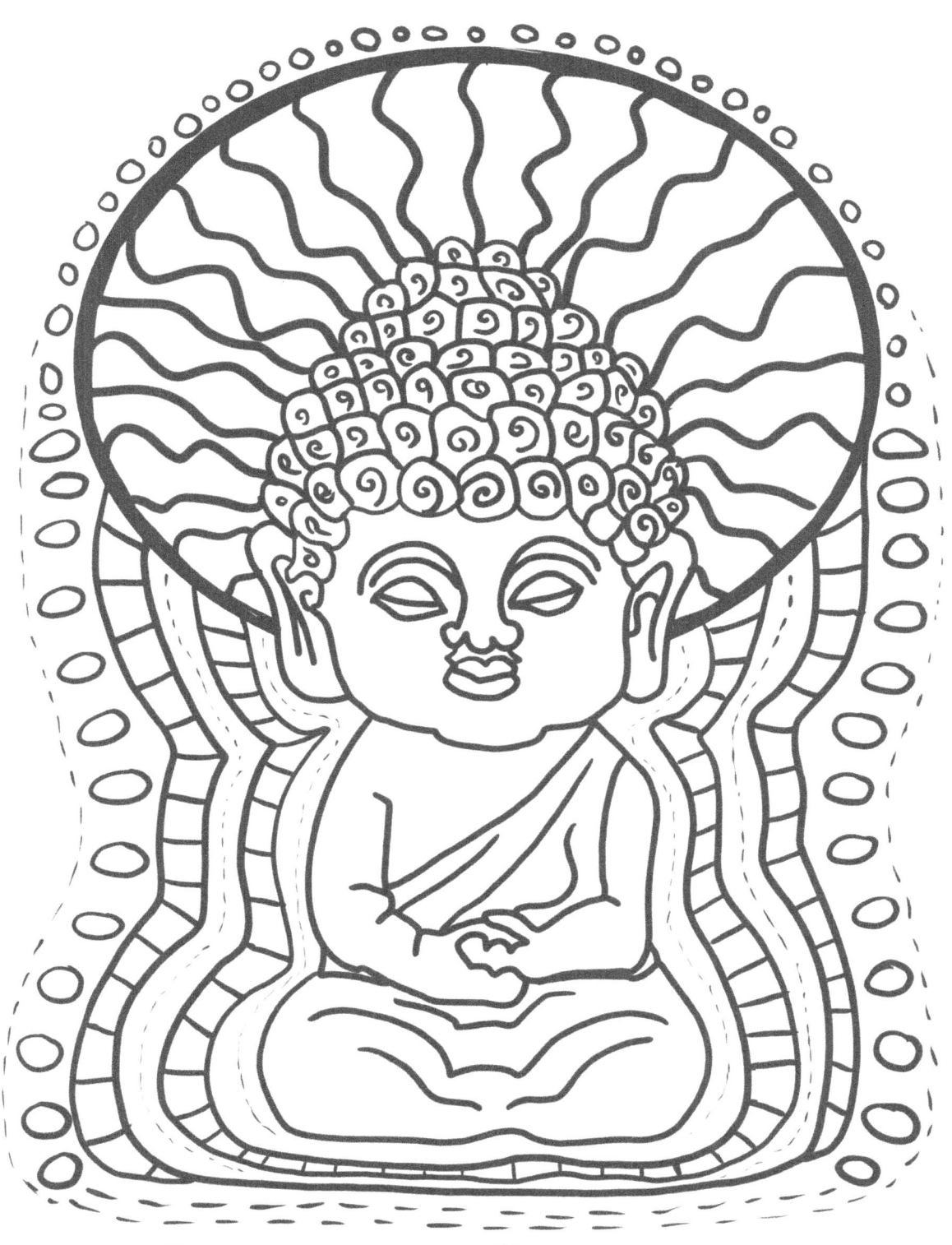

Awaken

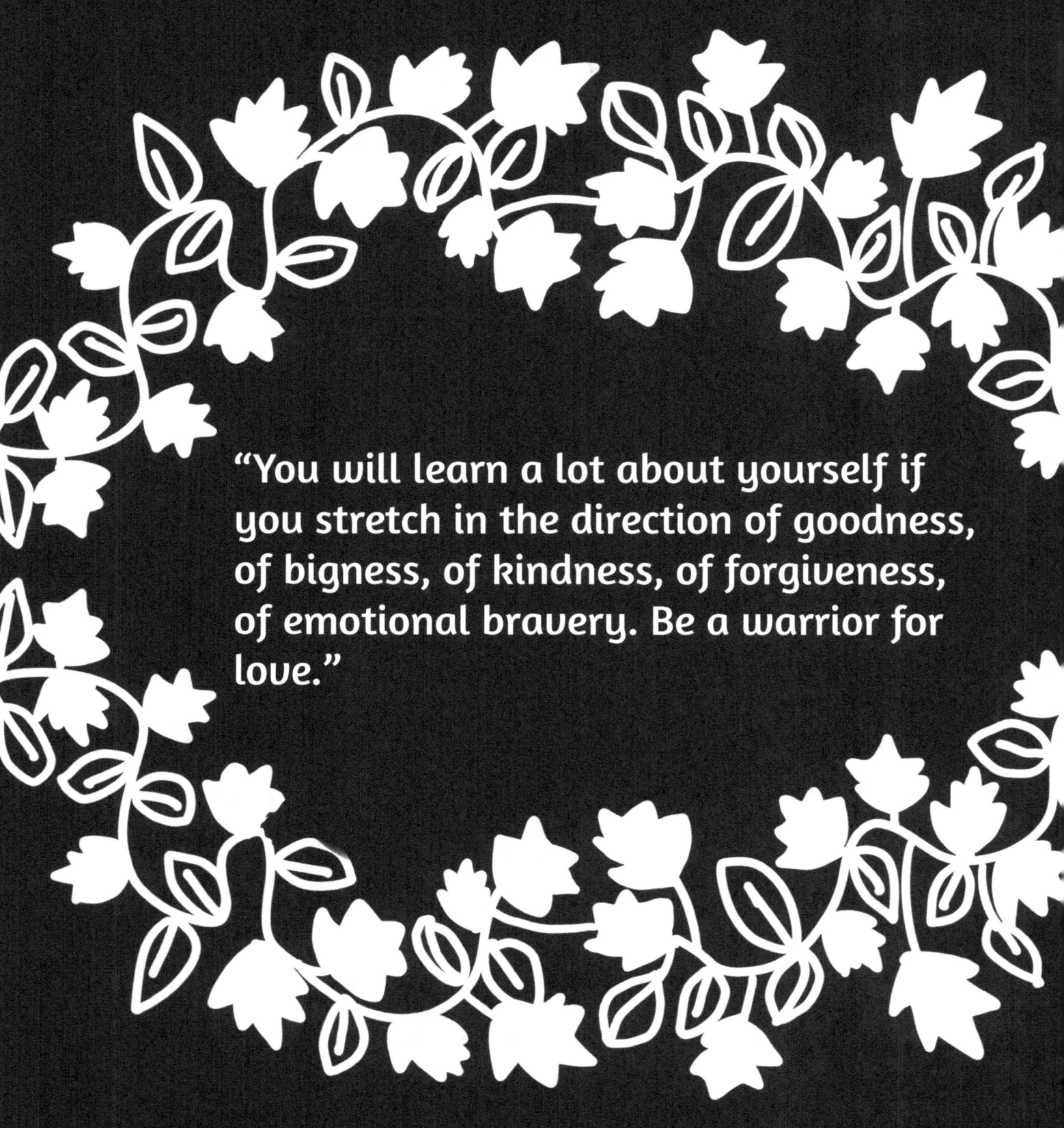

"You will learn a lot about yourself if you stretch in the direction of goodness, of bigness, of kindness, of forgiveness, of emotional bravery. Be a warrior for love."

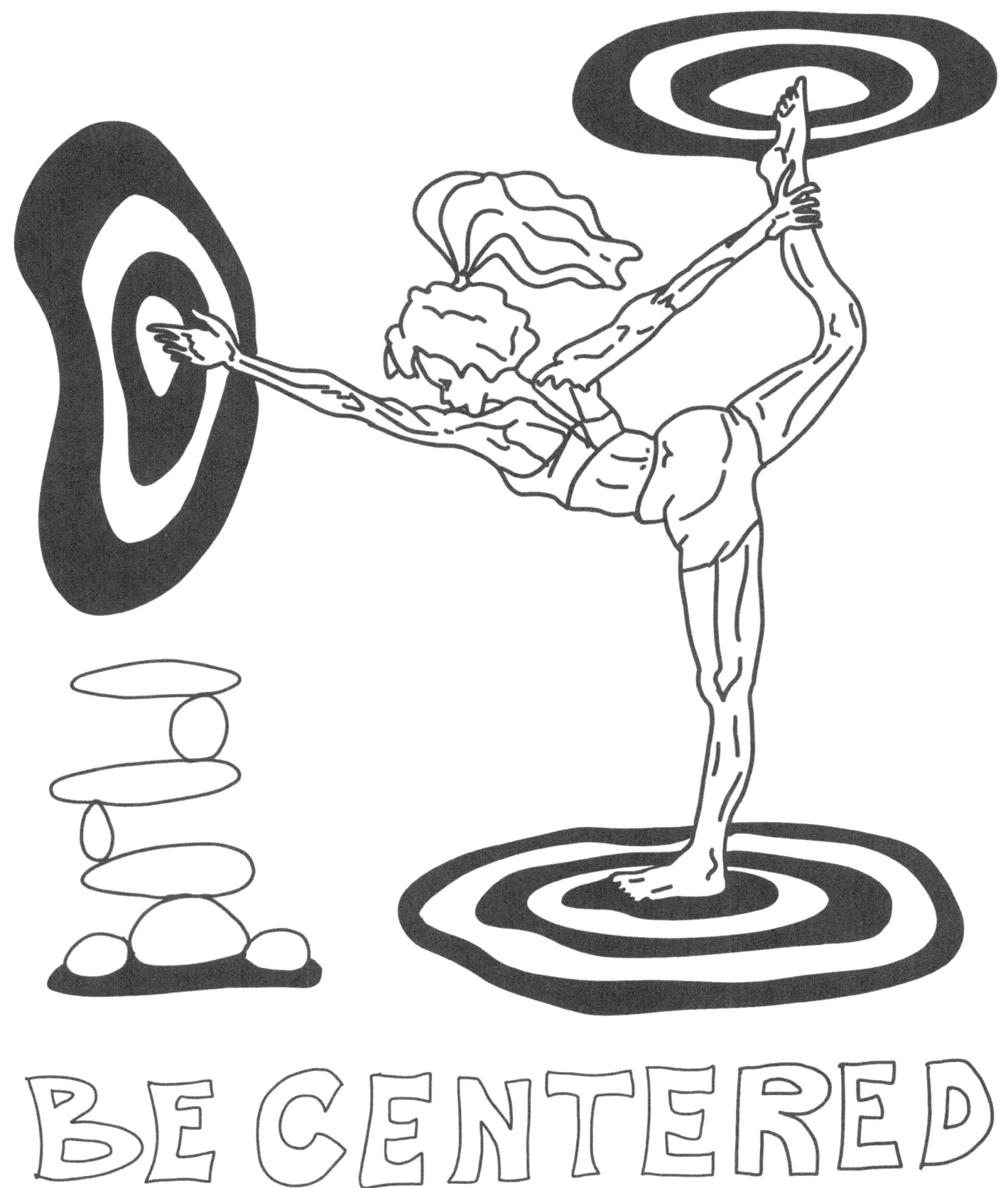

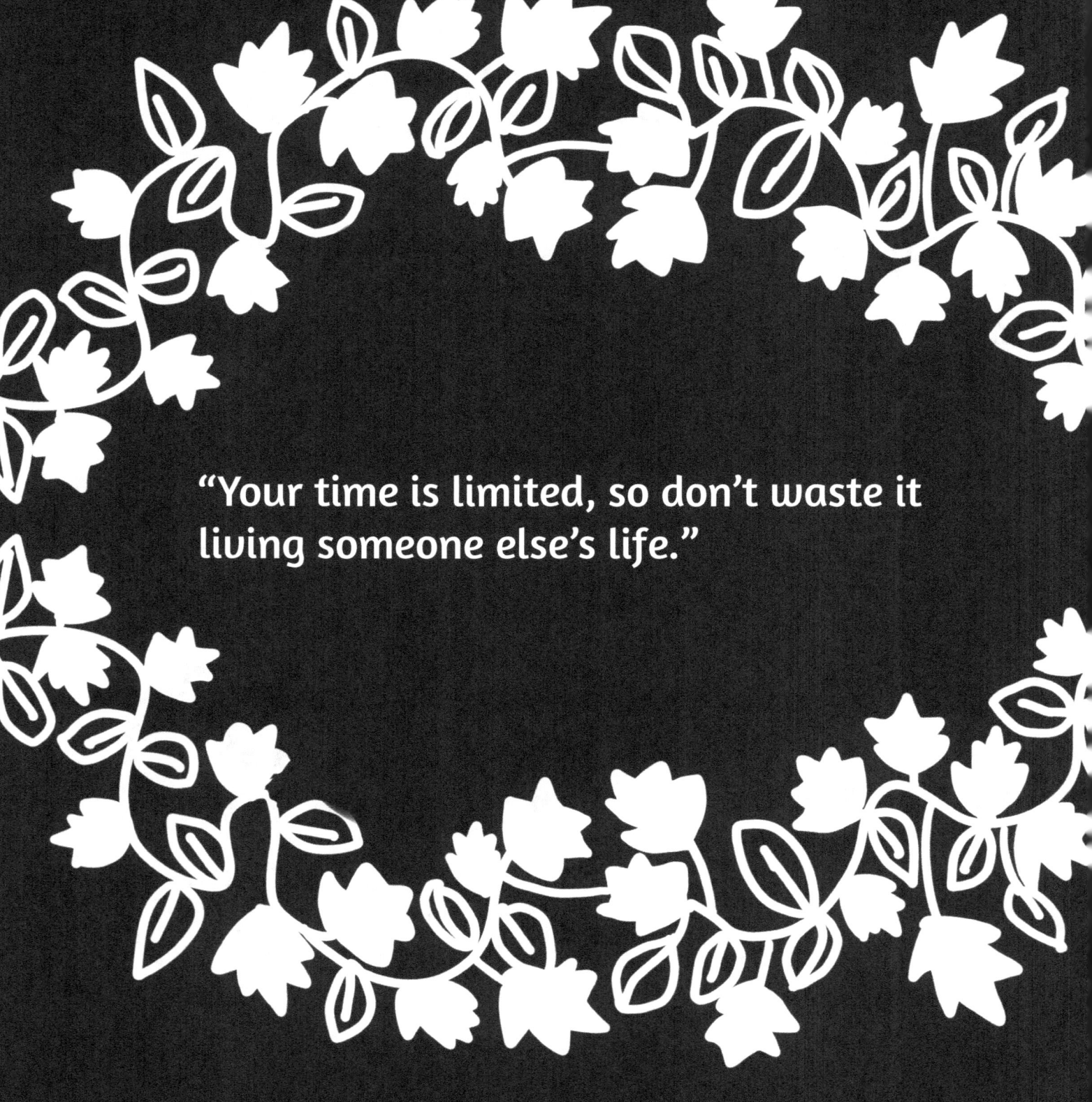

"Your time is limited, so don't waste it living someone else's life."

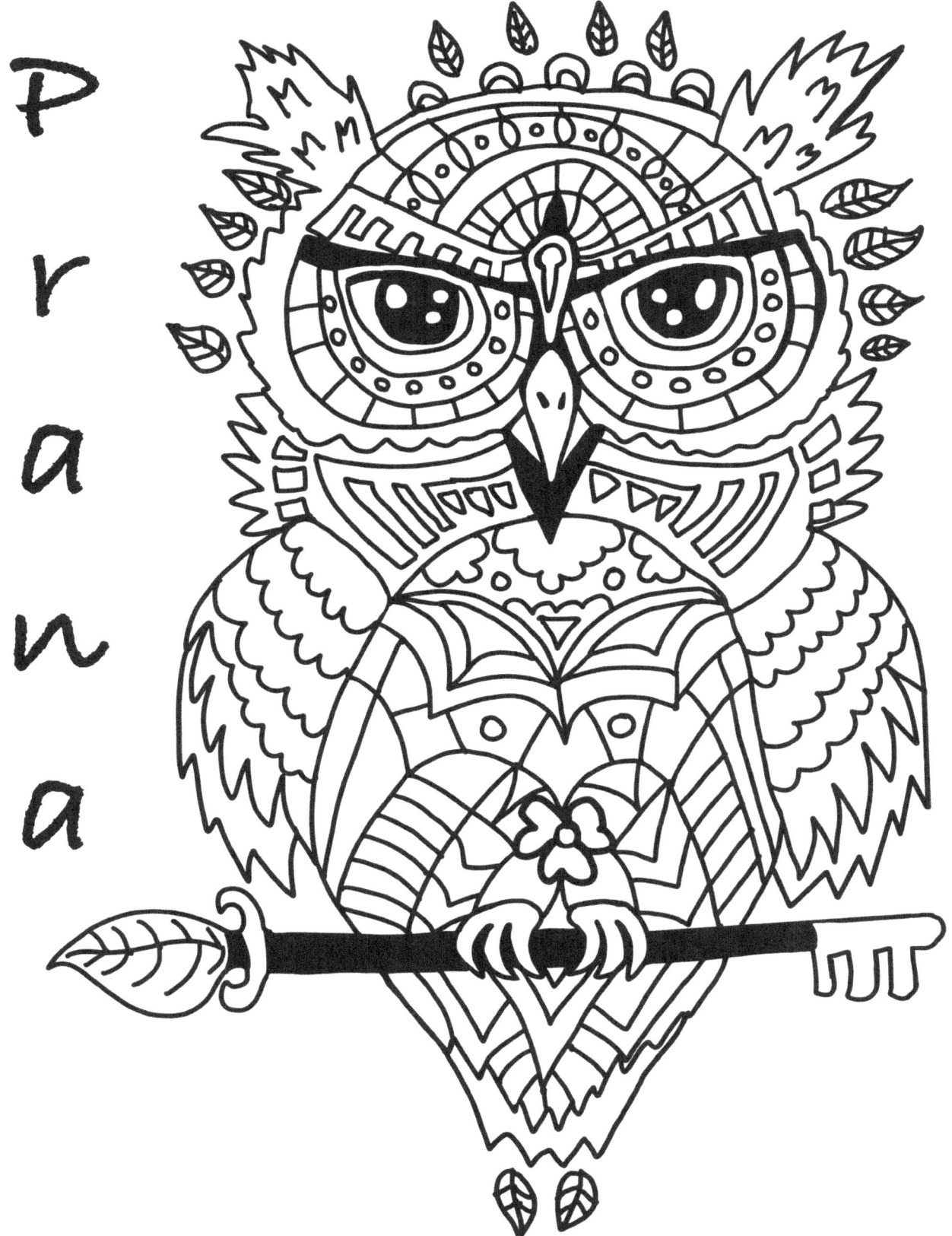

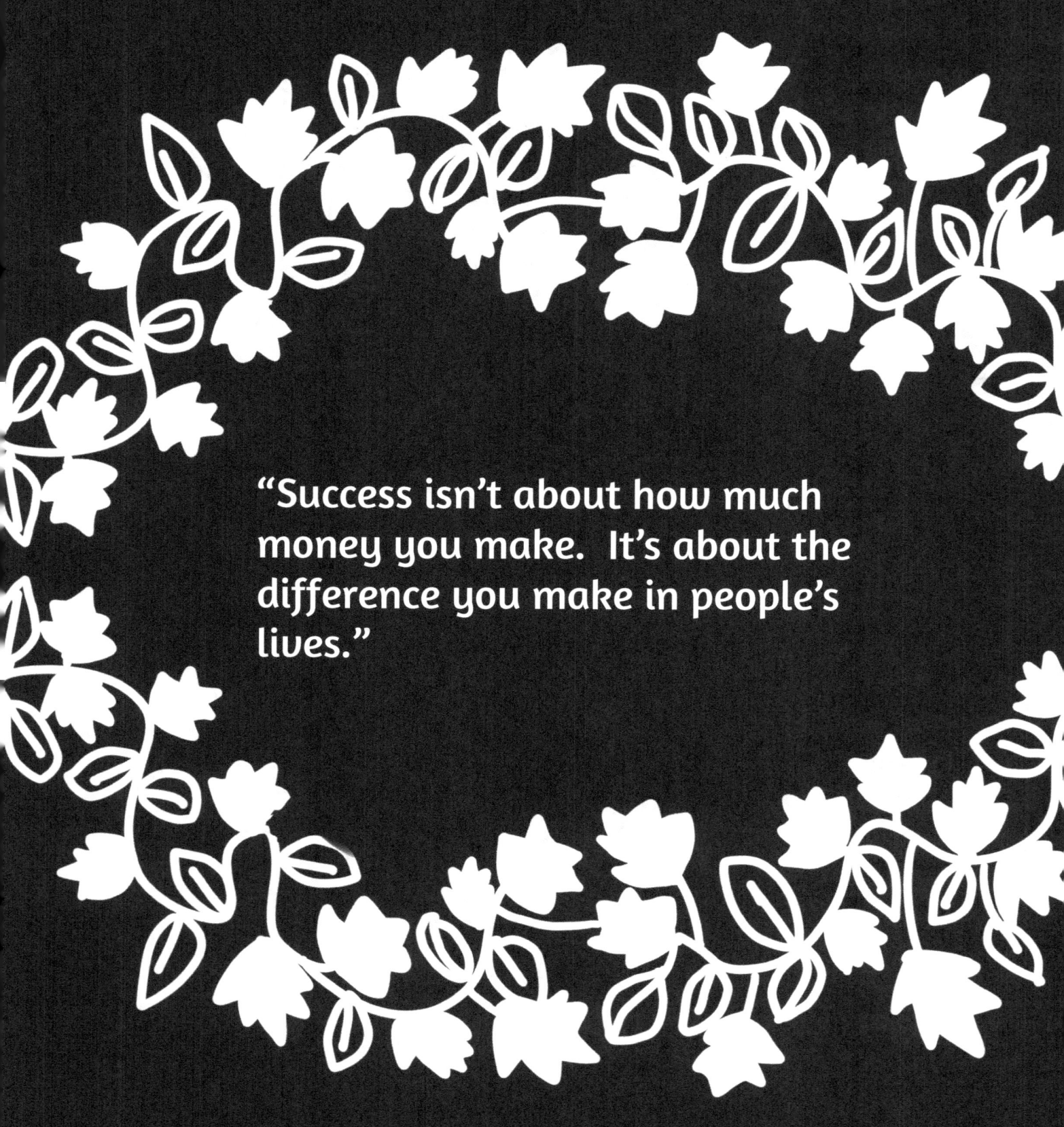

"Success isn't about how much money you make. It's about the difference you make in people's lives."

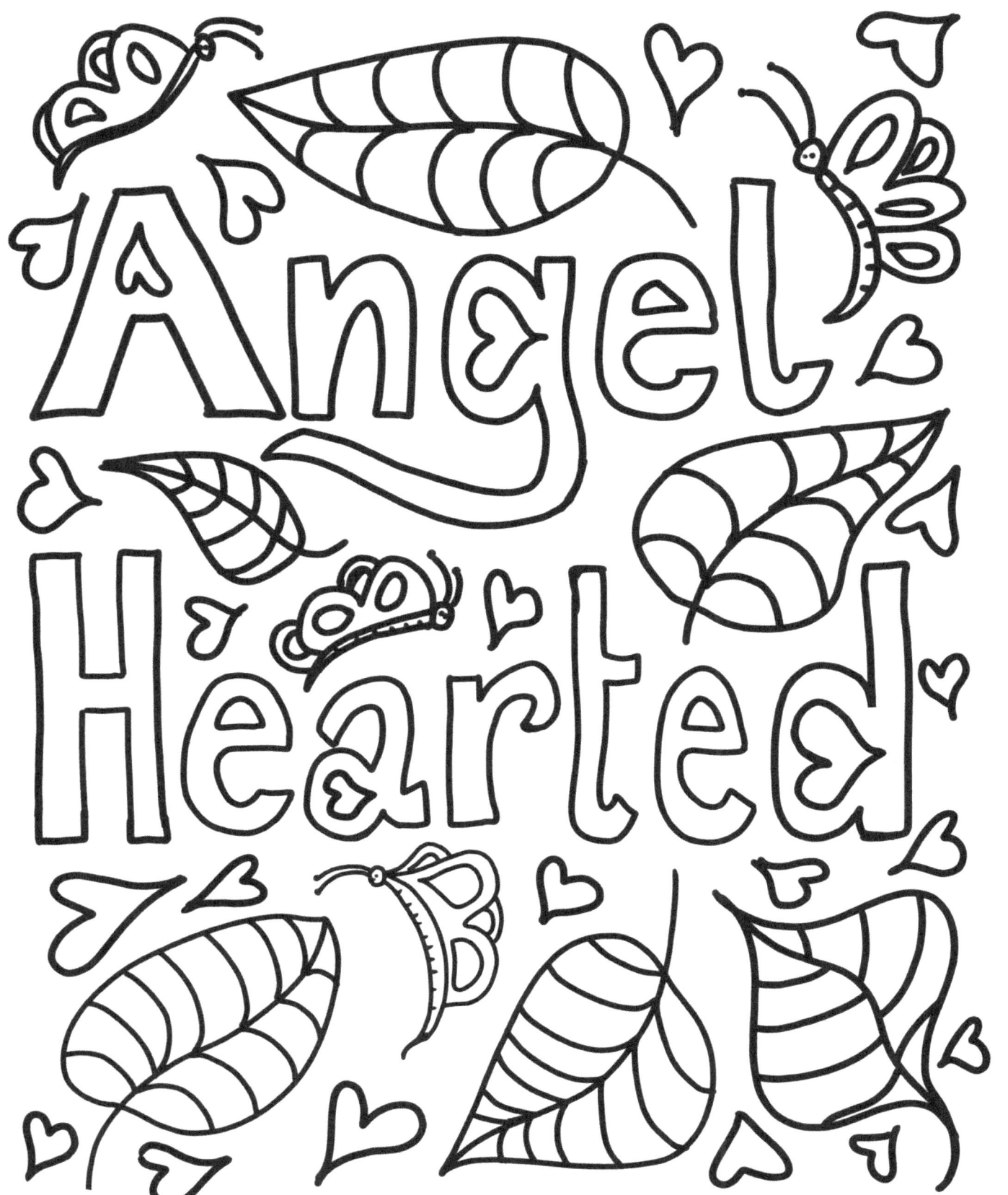

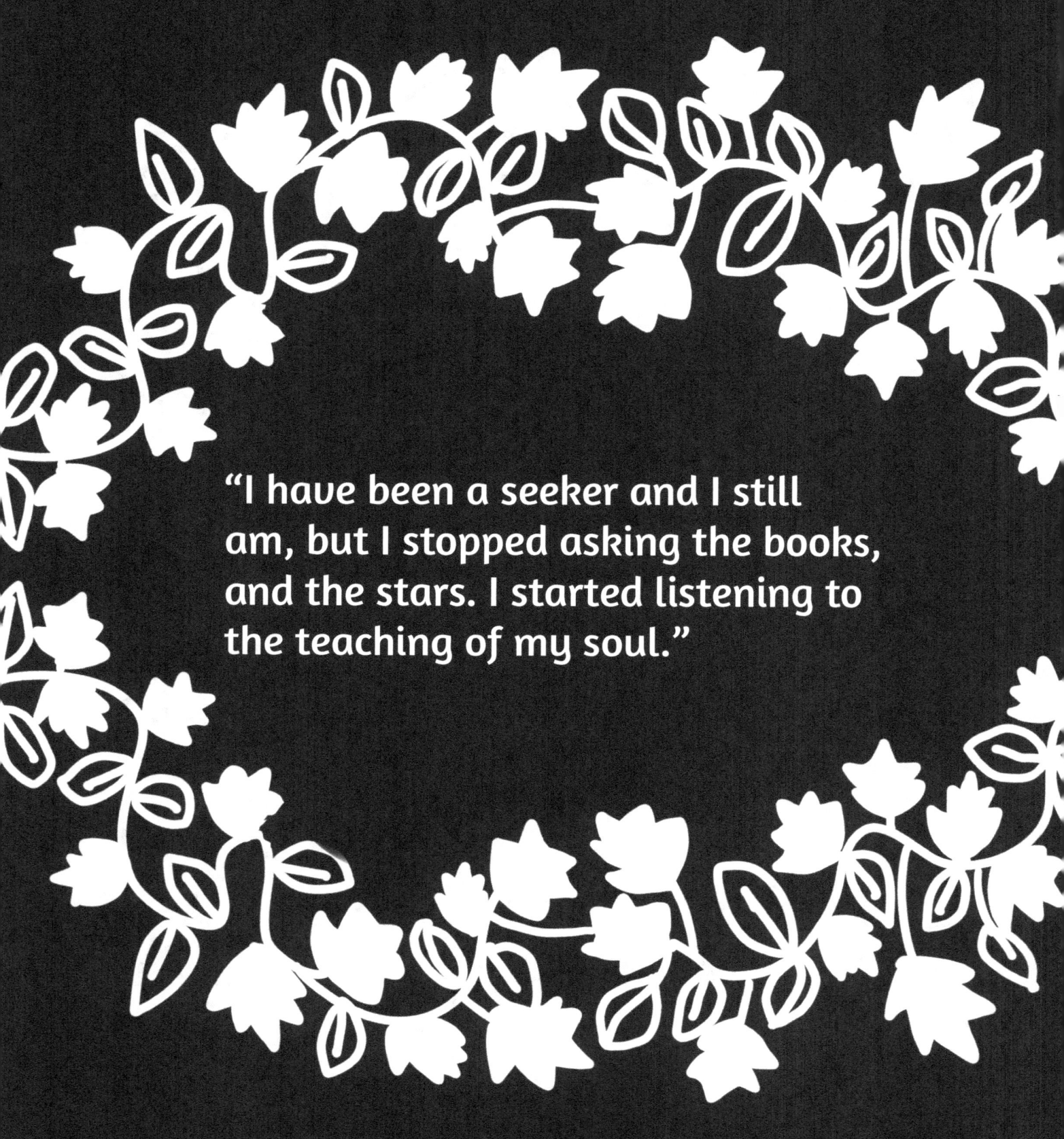

"I have been a seeker and I still am, but I stopped asking the books, and the stars. I started listening to the teaching of my soul."

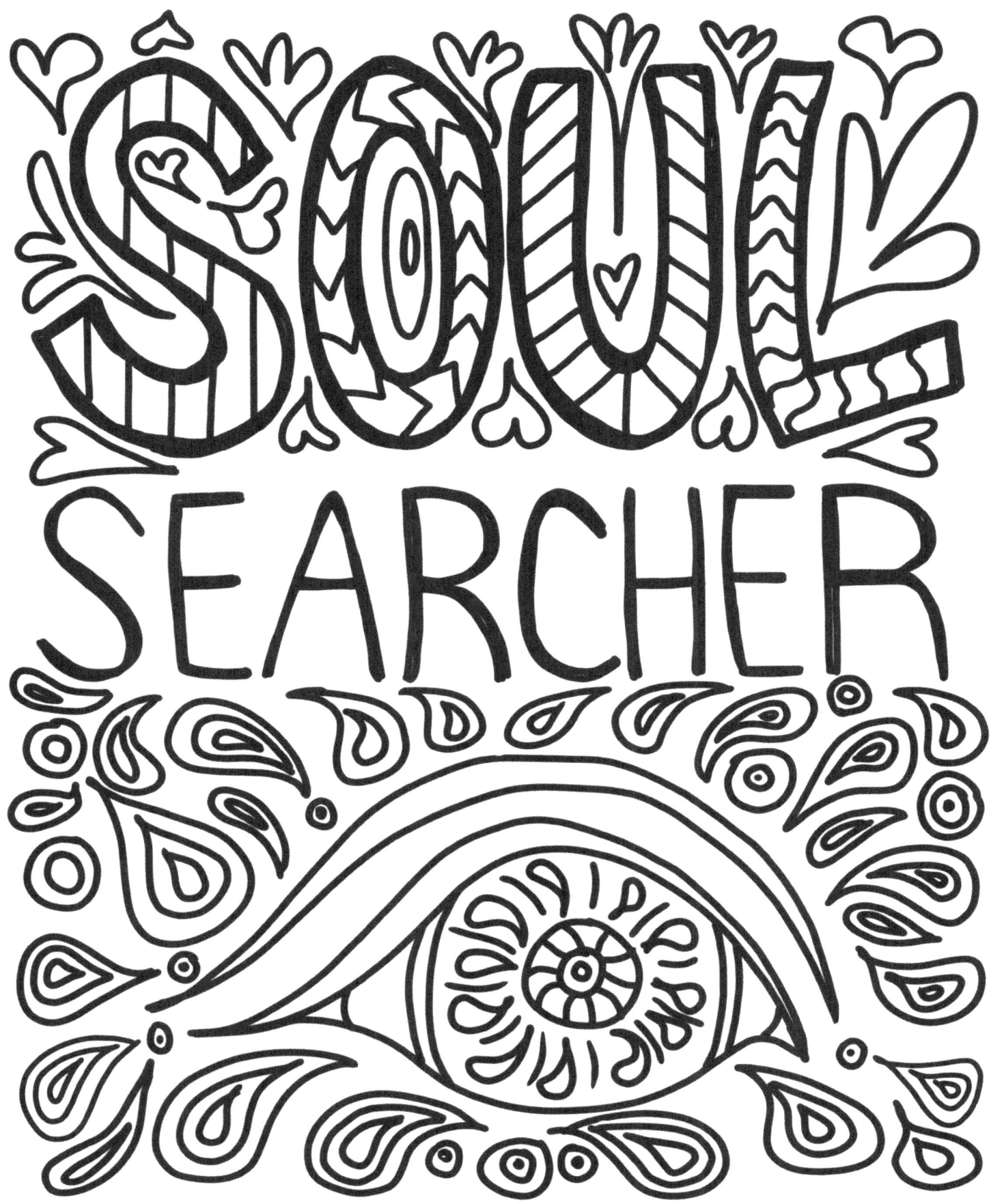

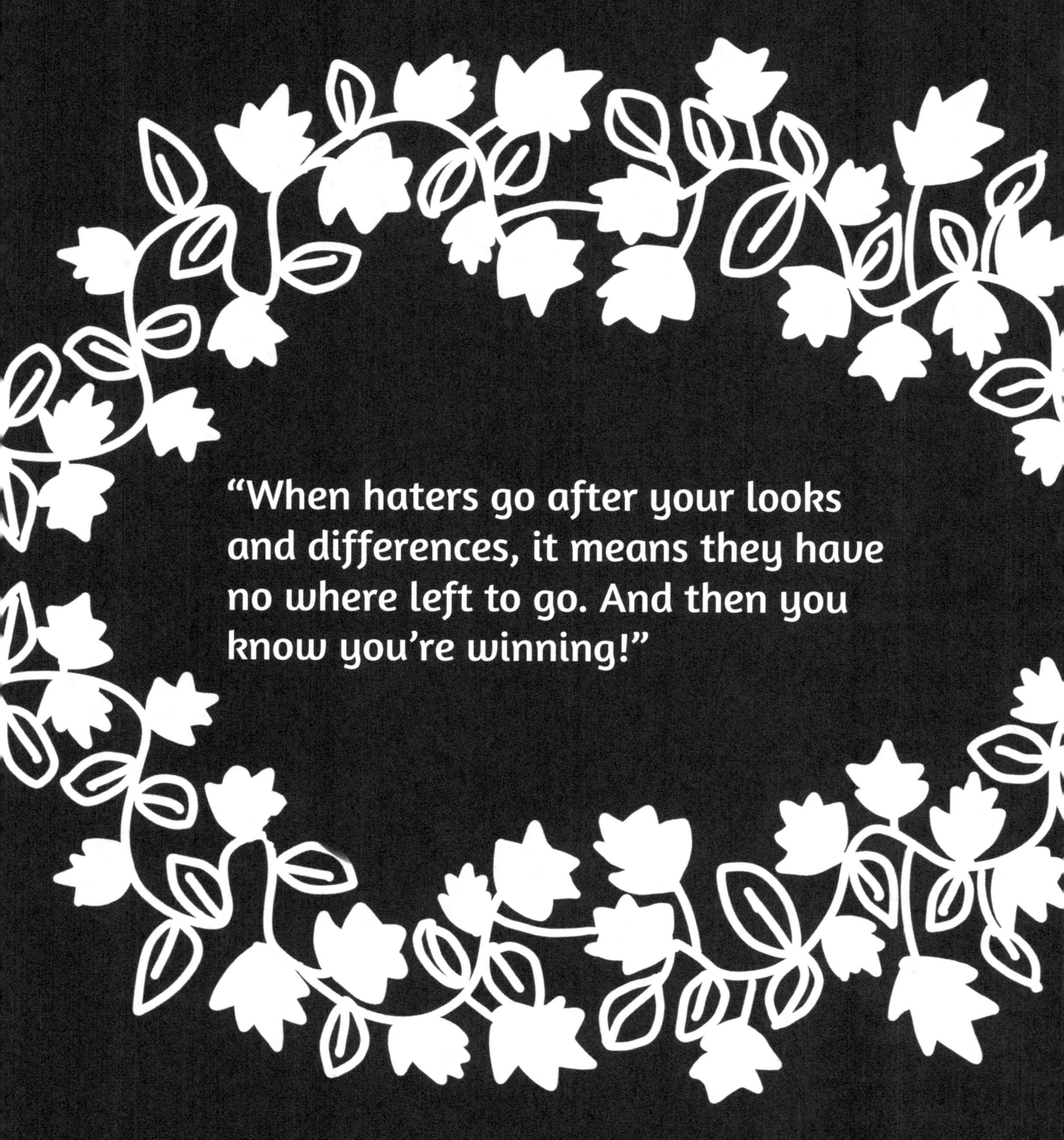

"When haters go after your looks and differences, it means they have no where left to go. And then you know you're winning!"

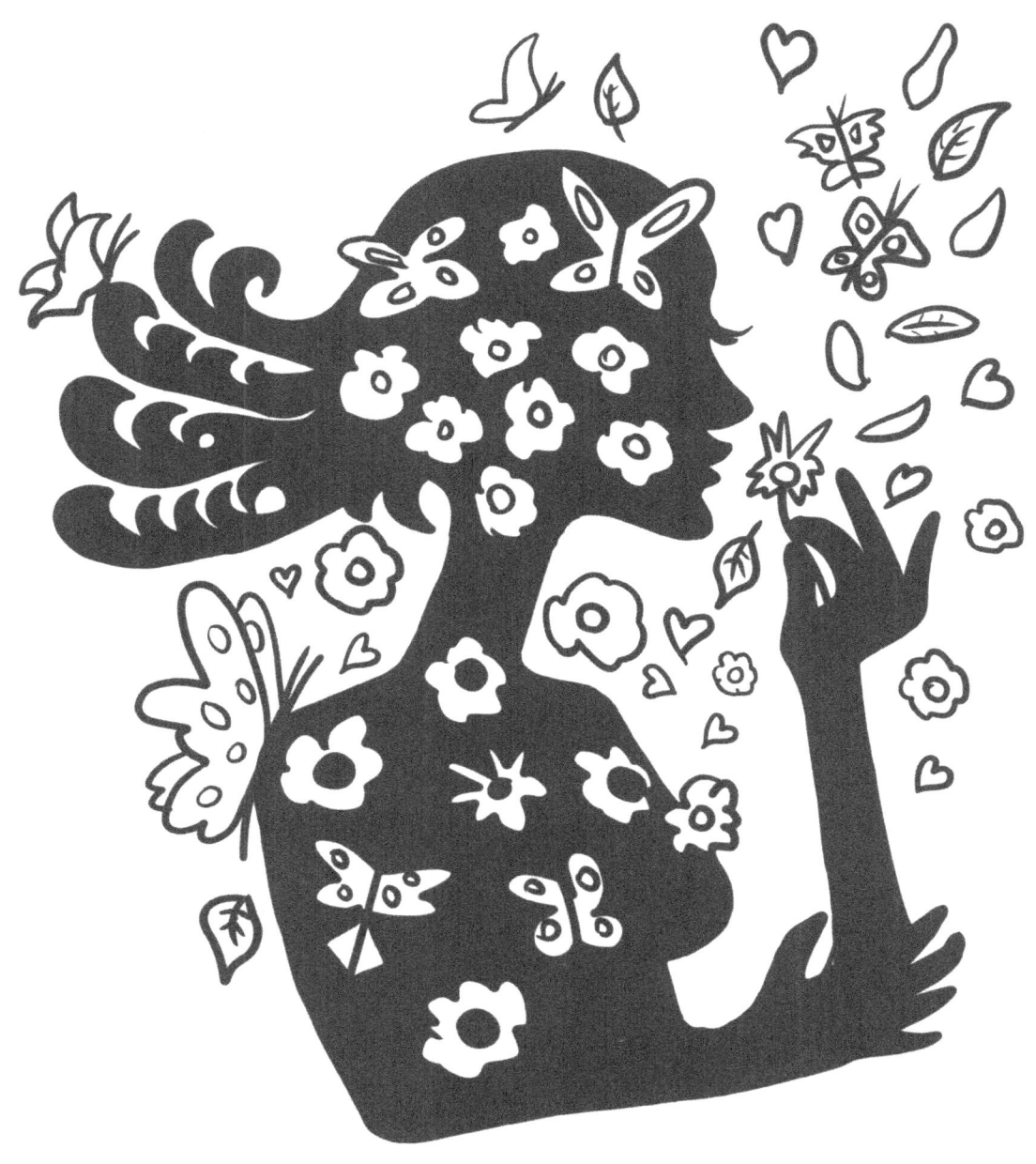

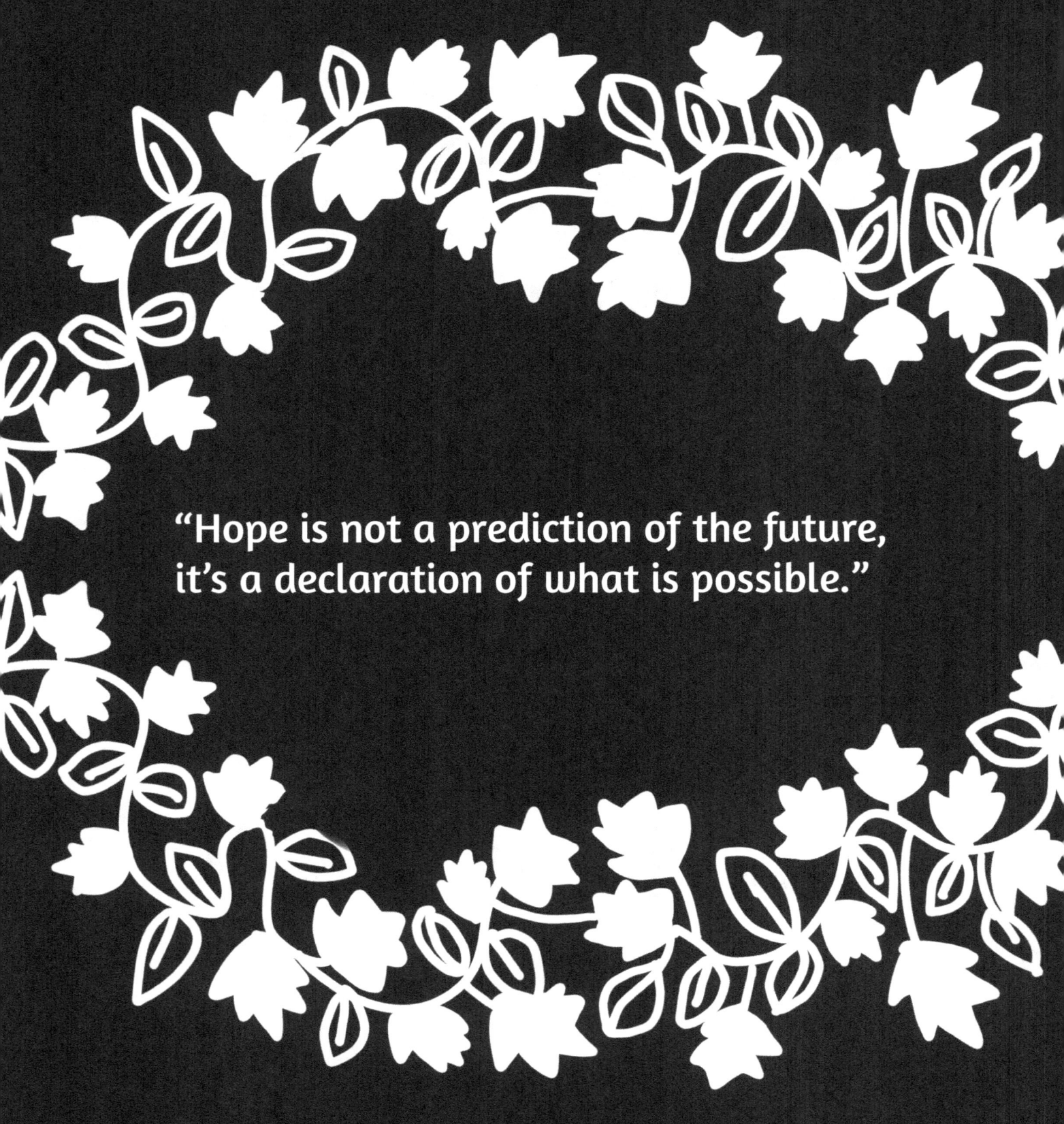

"Hope is not a prediction of the future, it's a declaration of what is possible."

Hamsa Amulet

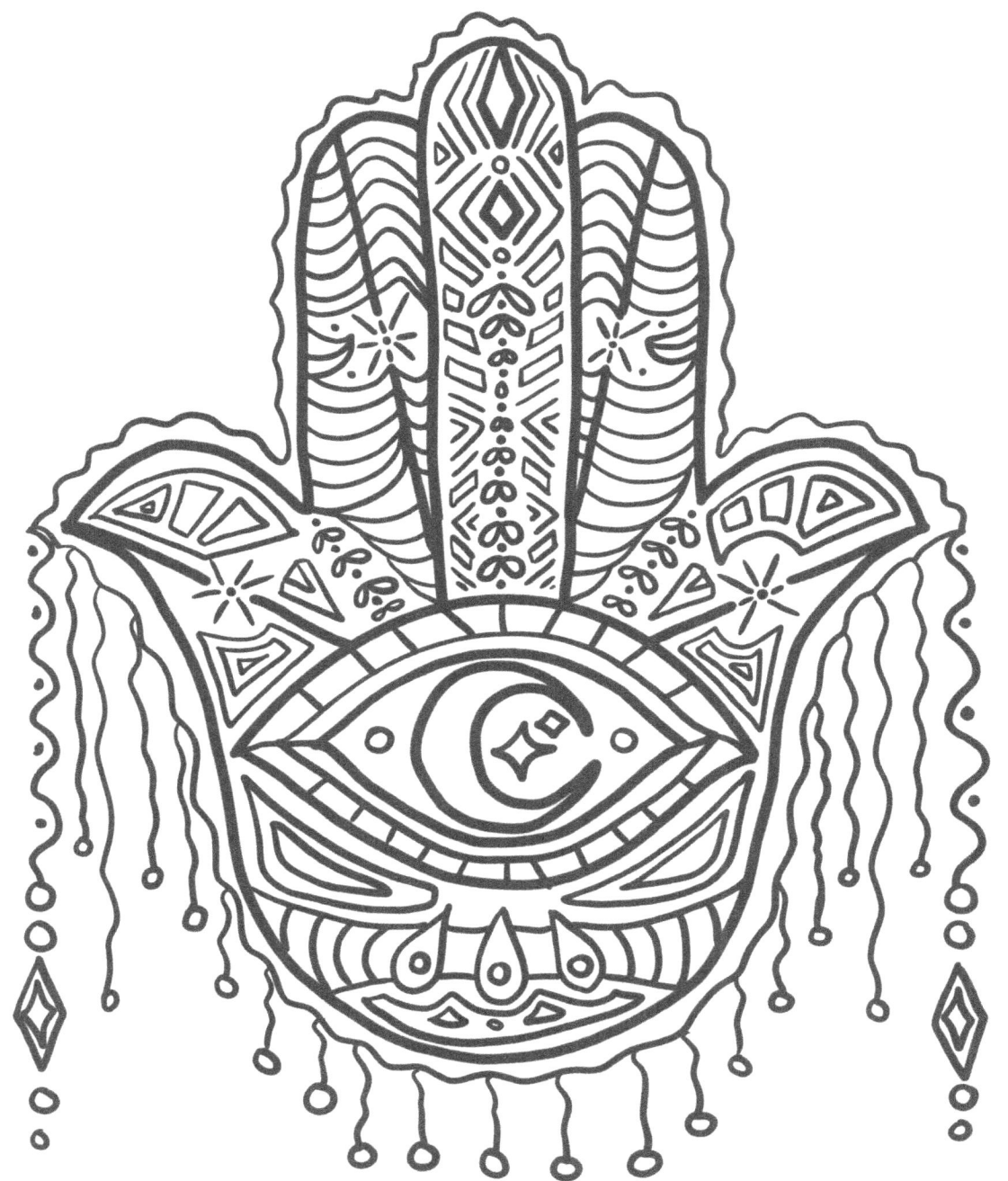

Protection

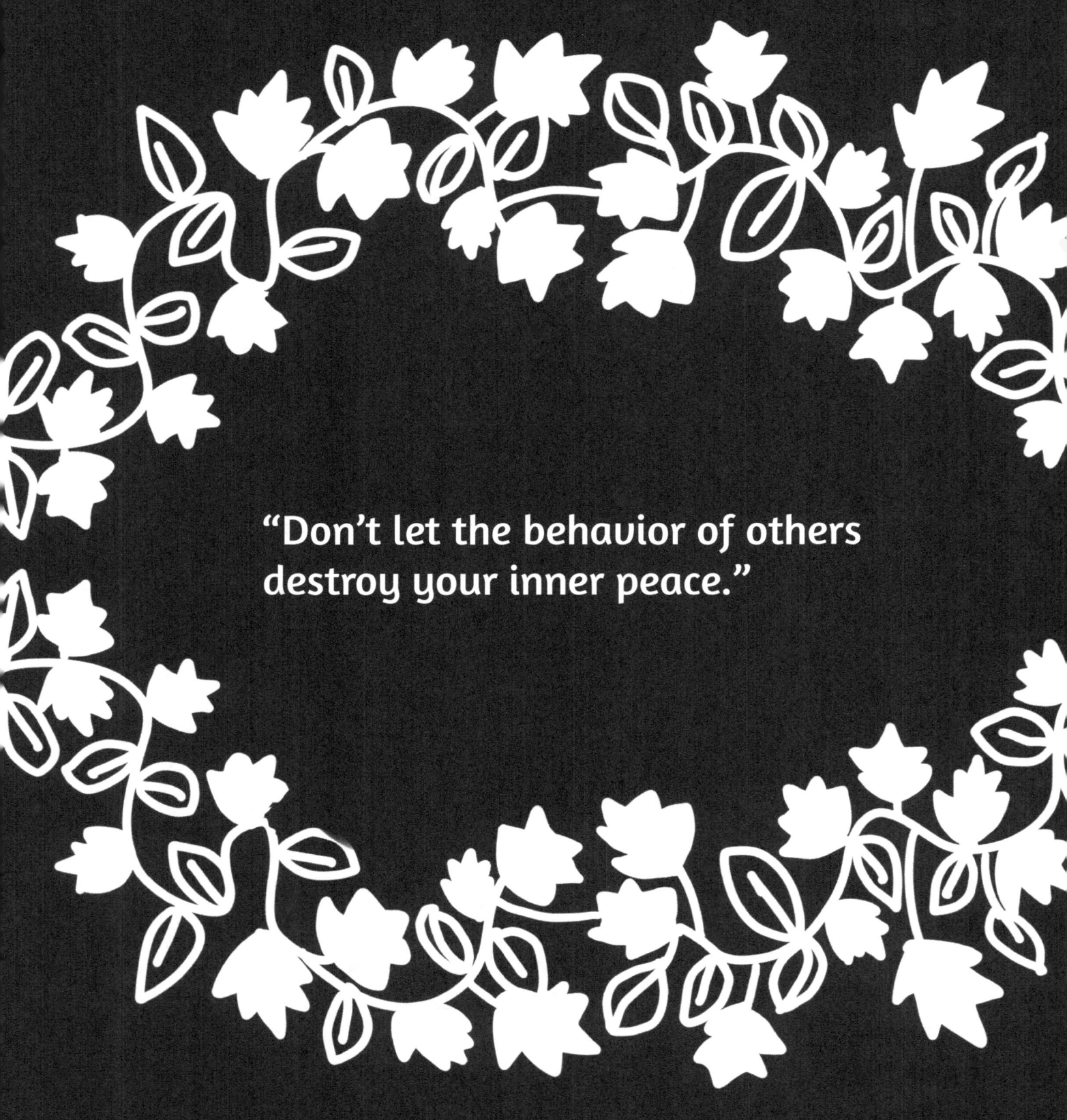

"Don't let the behavior of others destroy your inner peace."

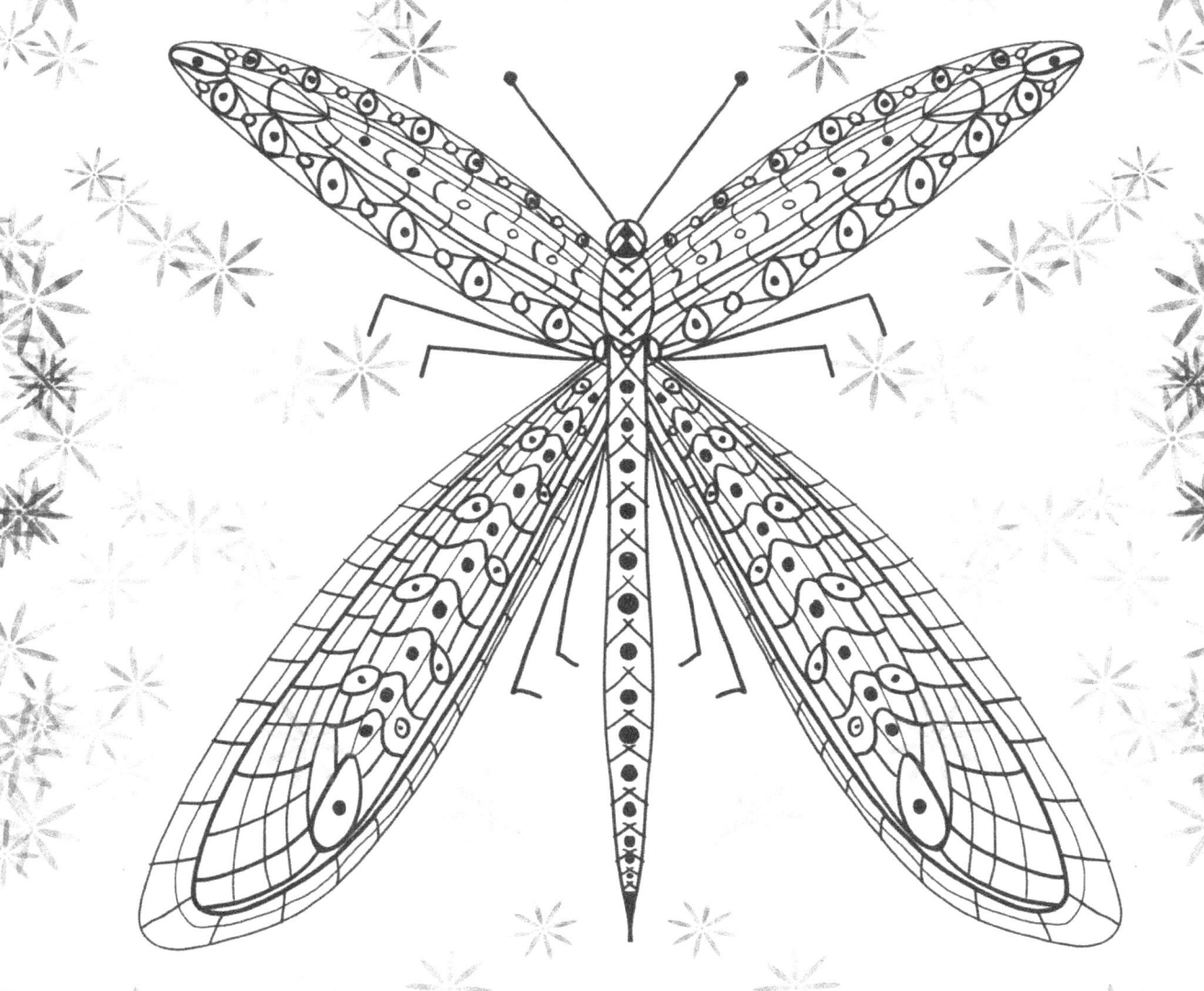

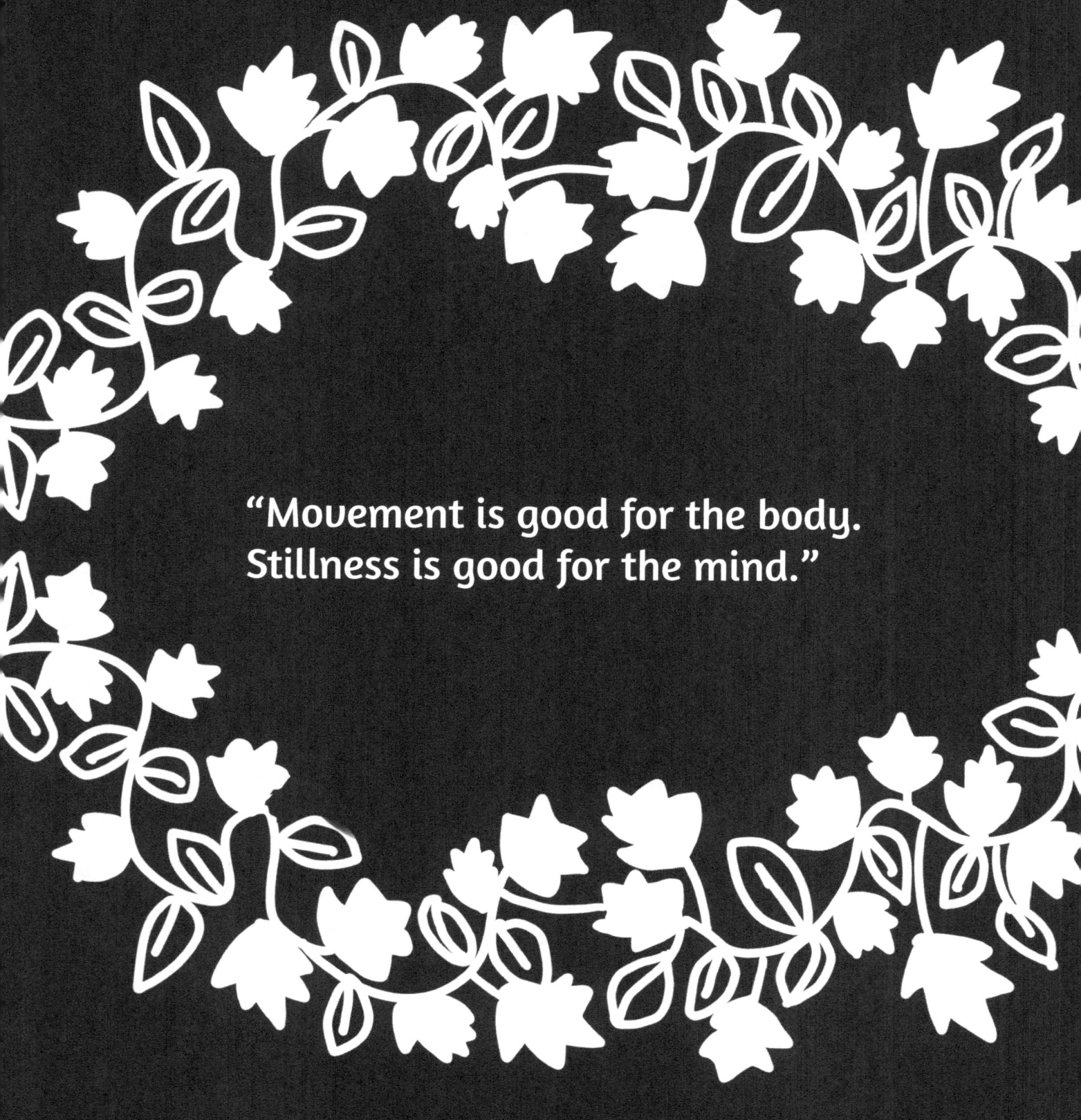

"Movement is good for the body. Stillness is good for the mind."

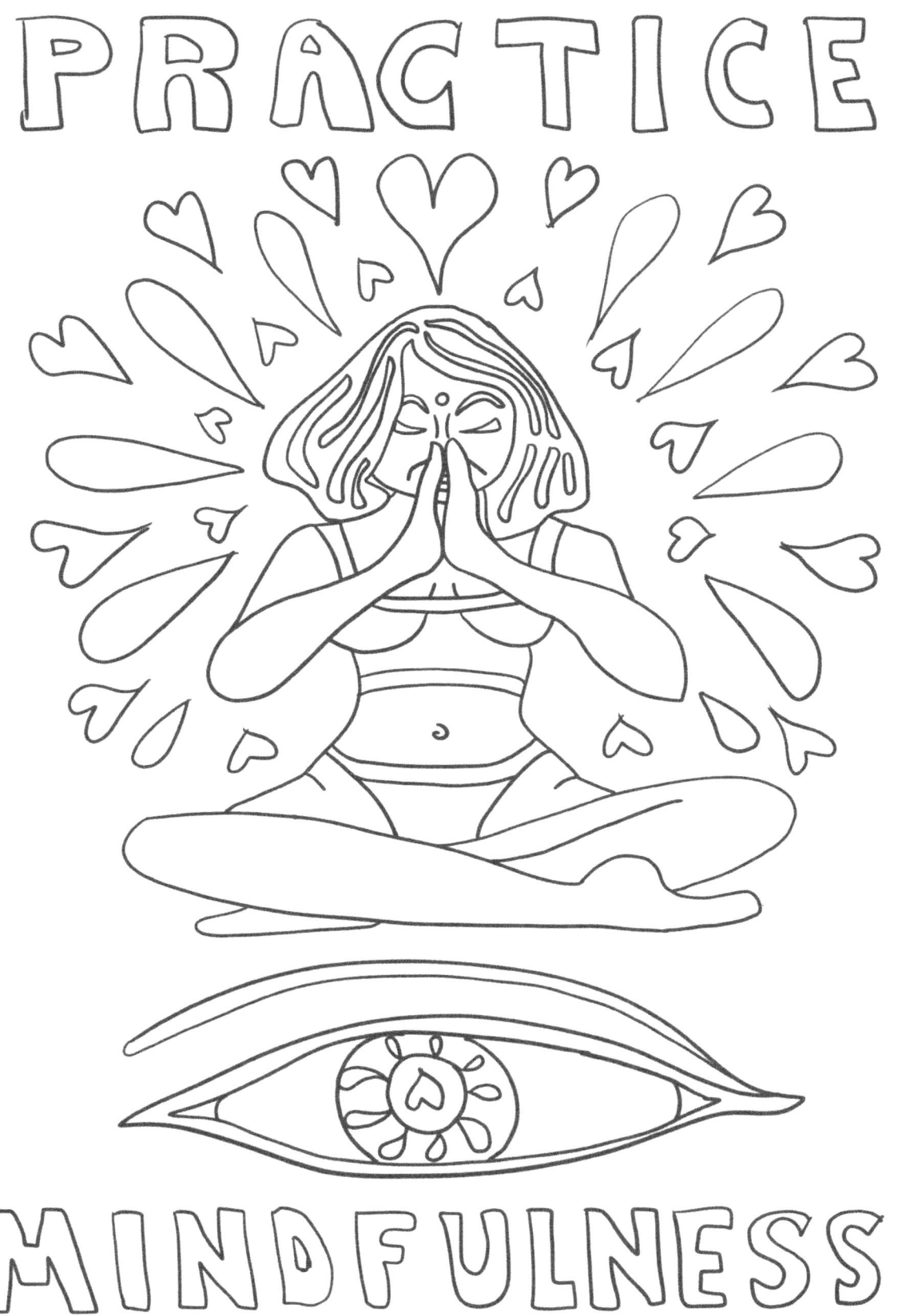

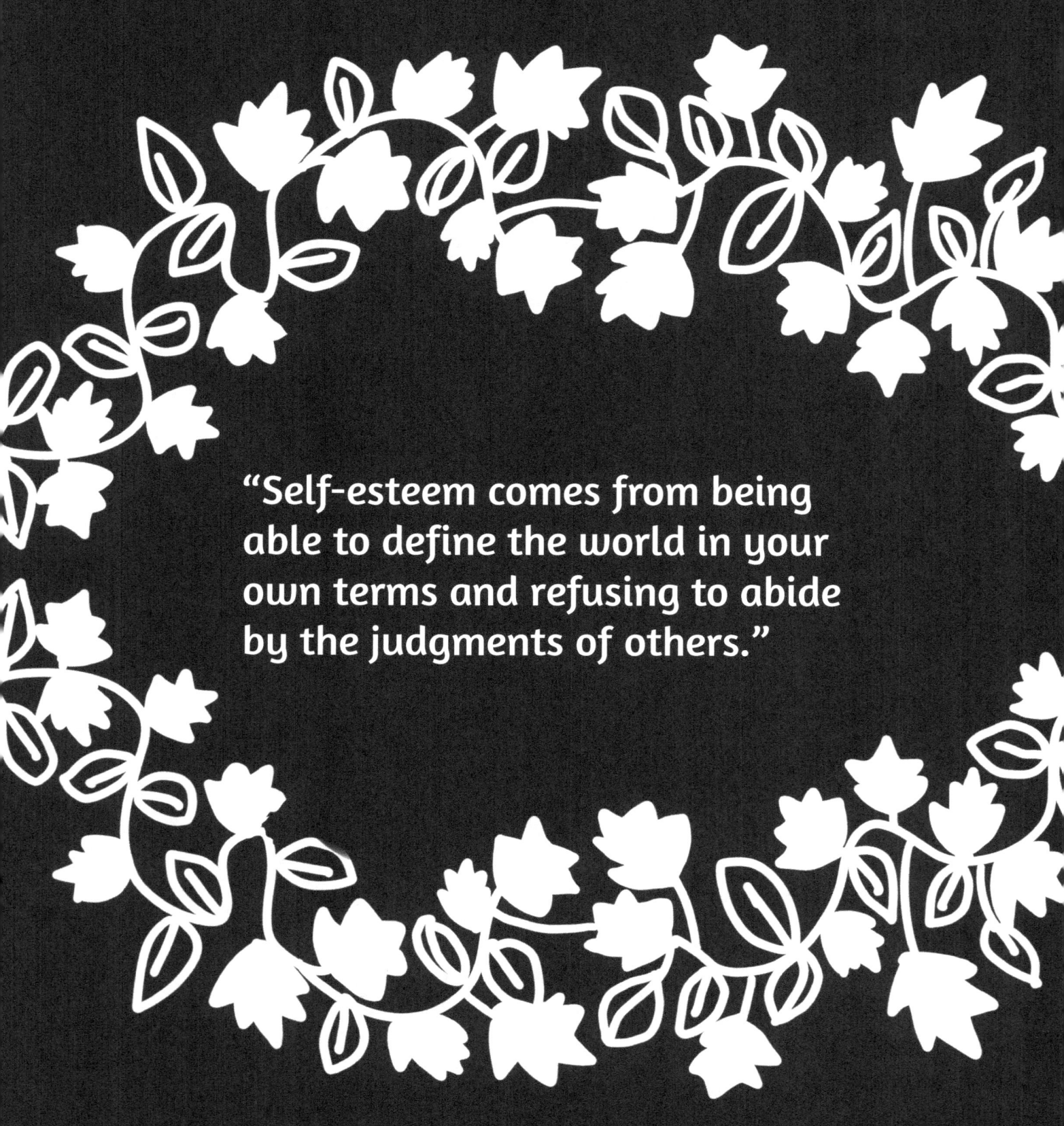

"Self-esteem comes from being able to define the world in your own terms and refusing to abide by the judgments of others."

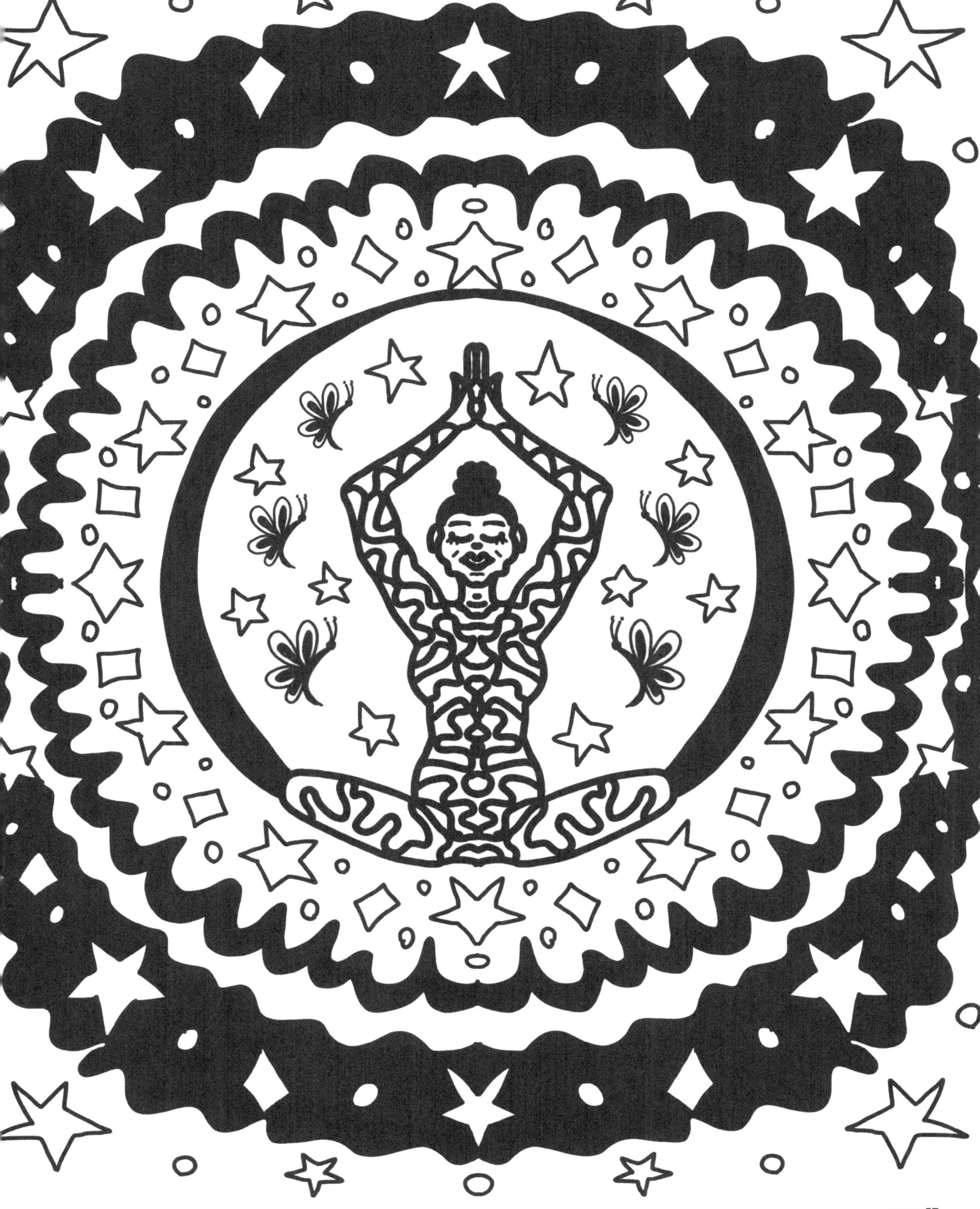

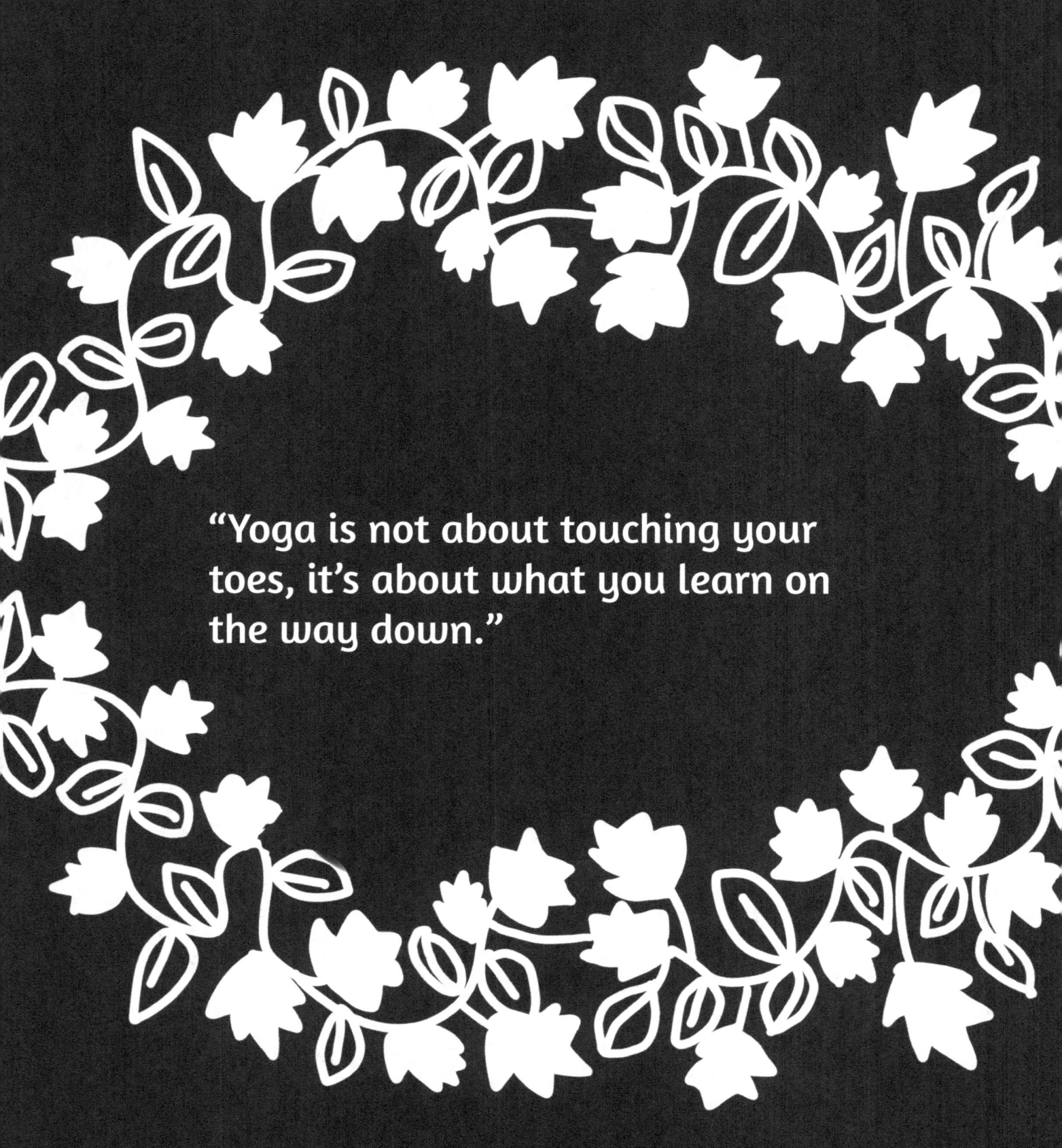

"Yoga is not about touching your toes, it's about what you learn on the way down."

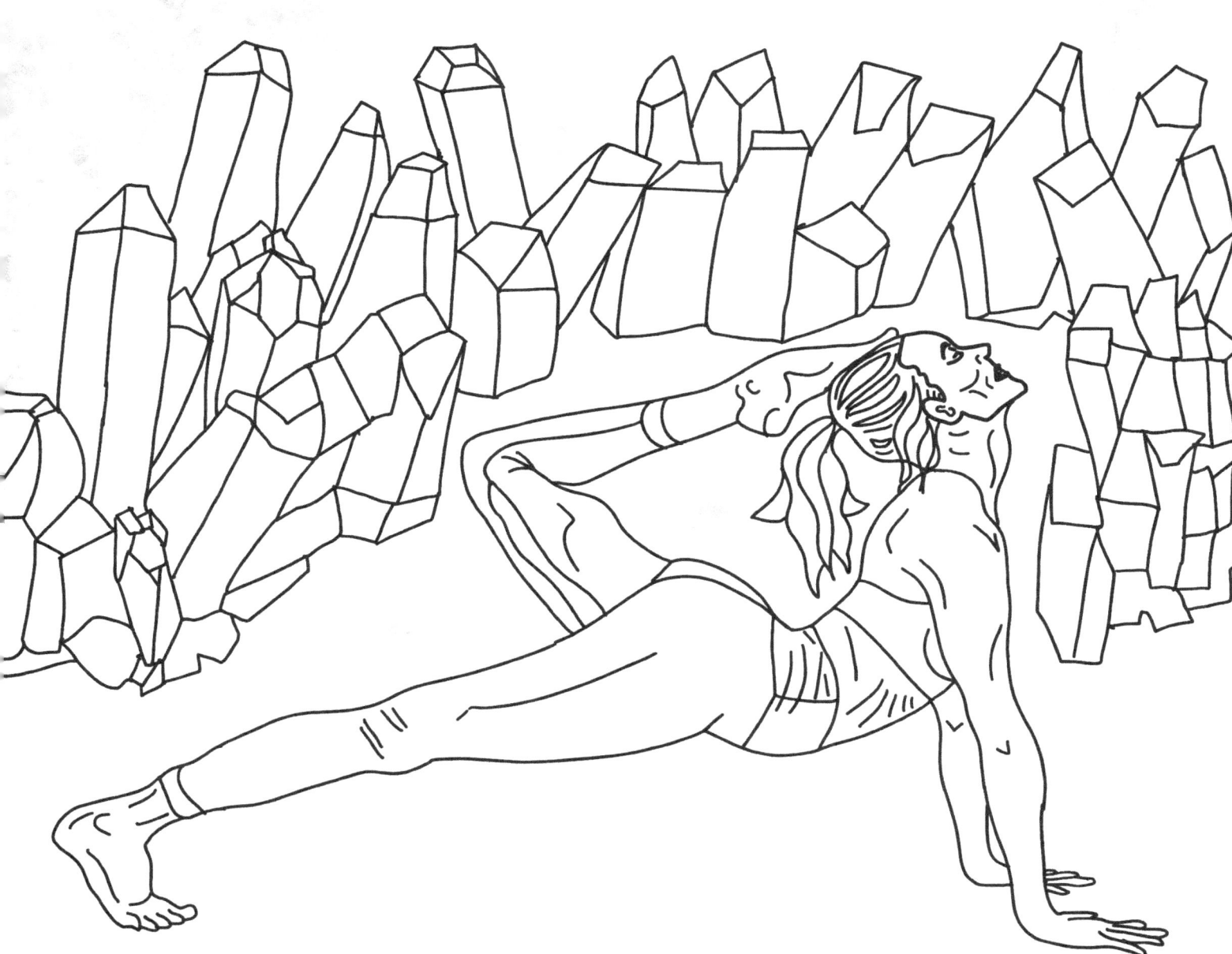

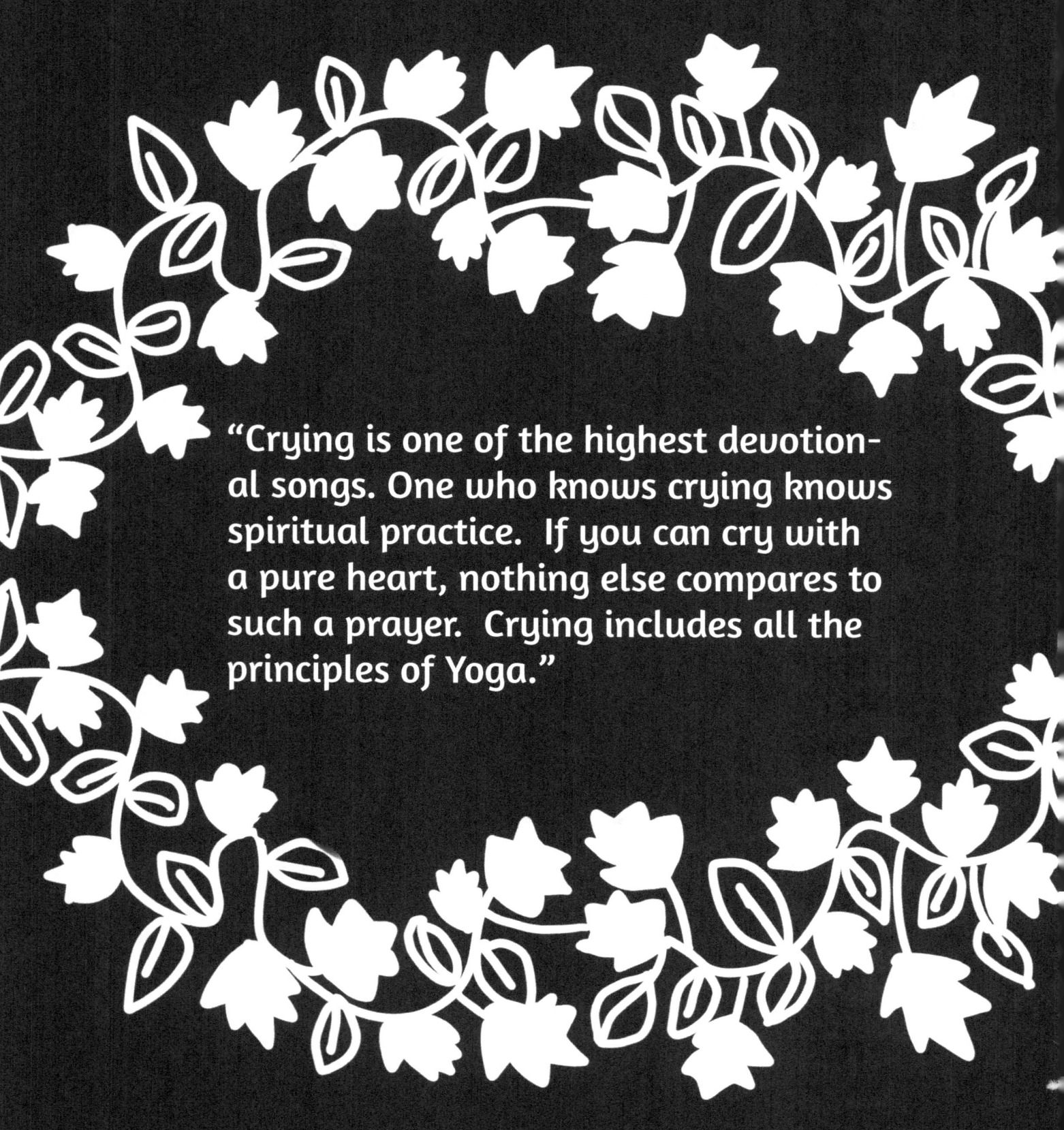

"Crying is one of the highest devotional songs. One who knows crying knows spiritual practice. If you can cry with a pure heart, nothing else compares to such a prayer. Crying includes all the principles of Yoga."

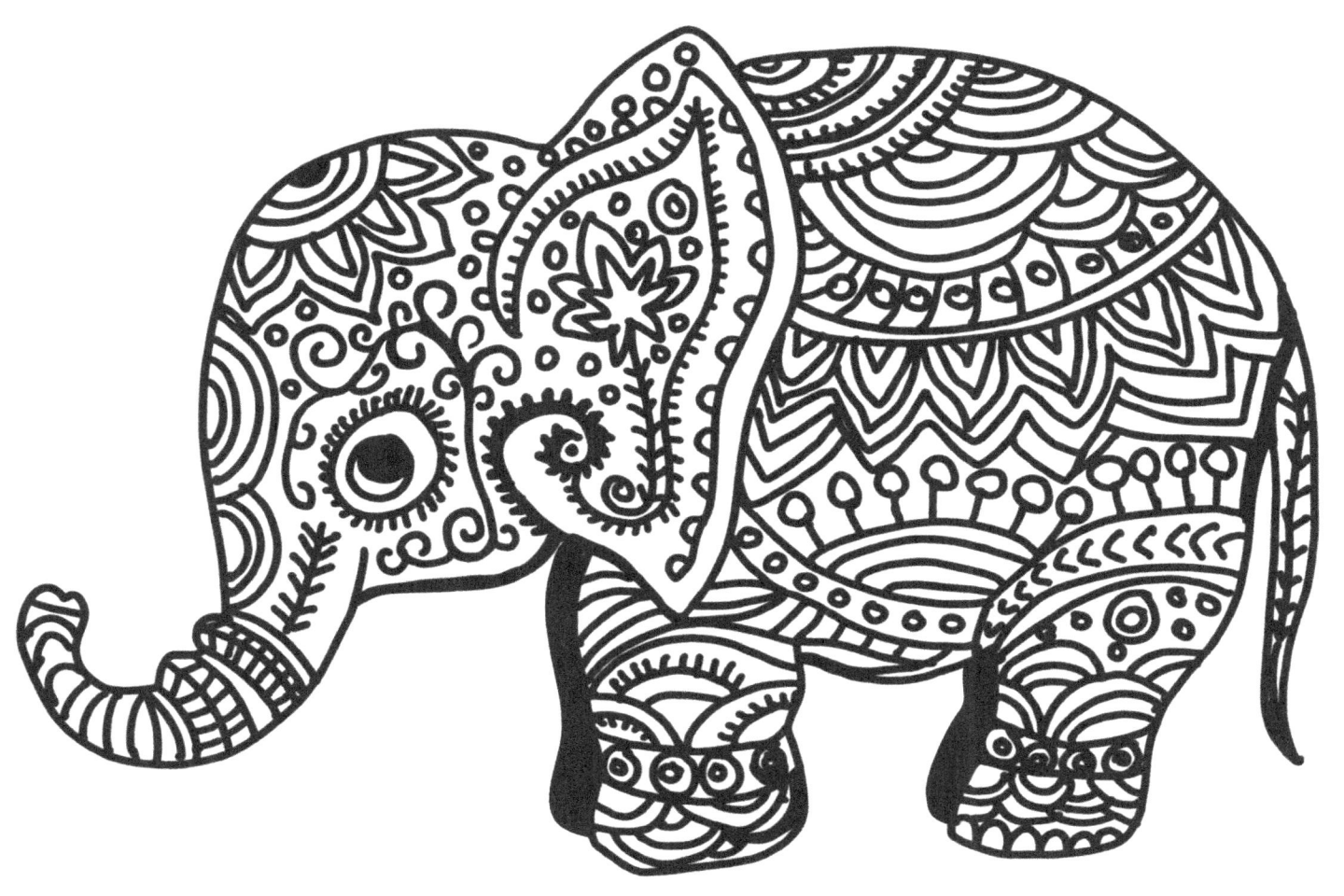

LOTUS SPIRIT

"I am rooted, but I flow."

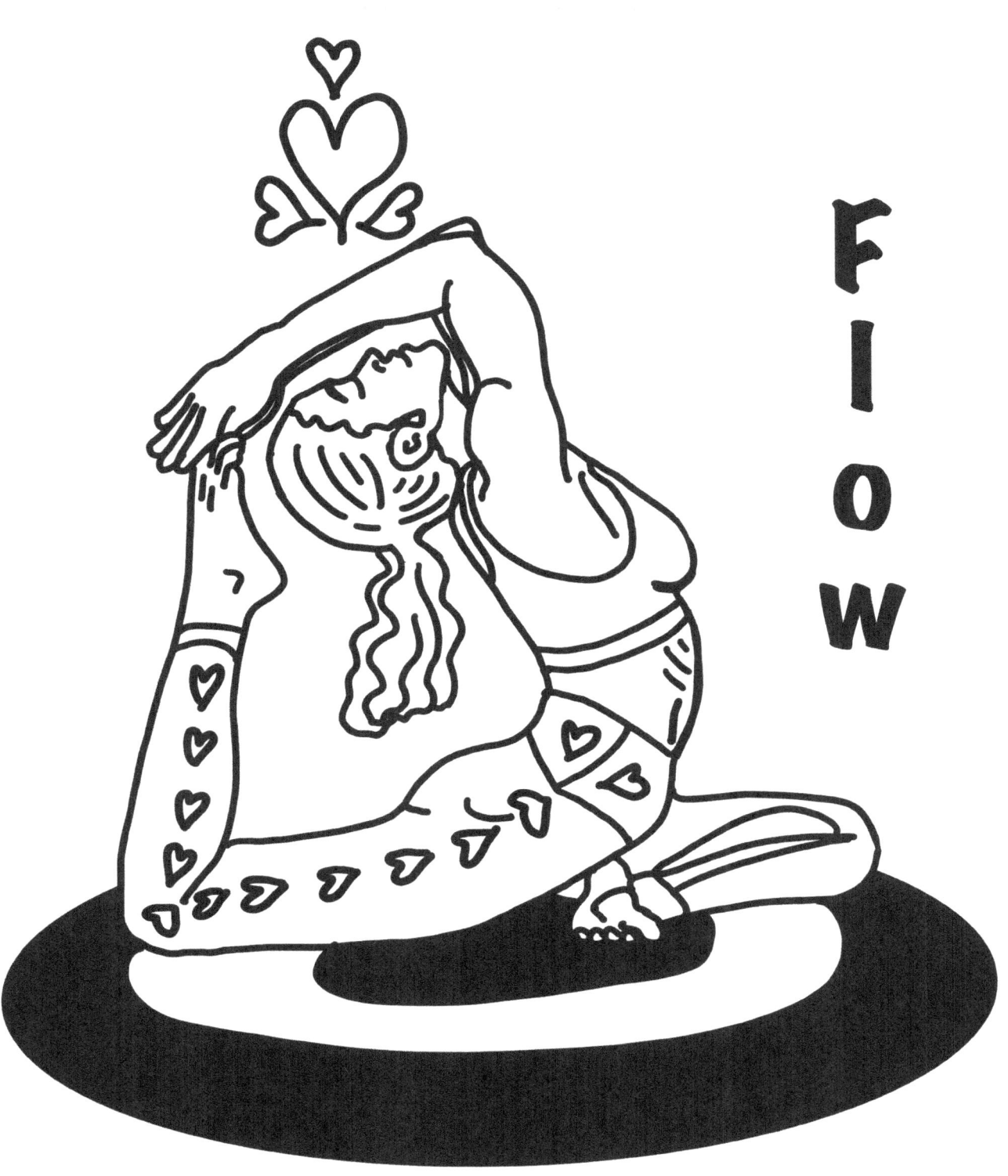

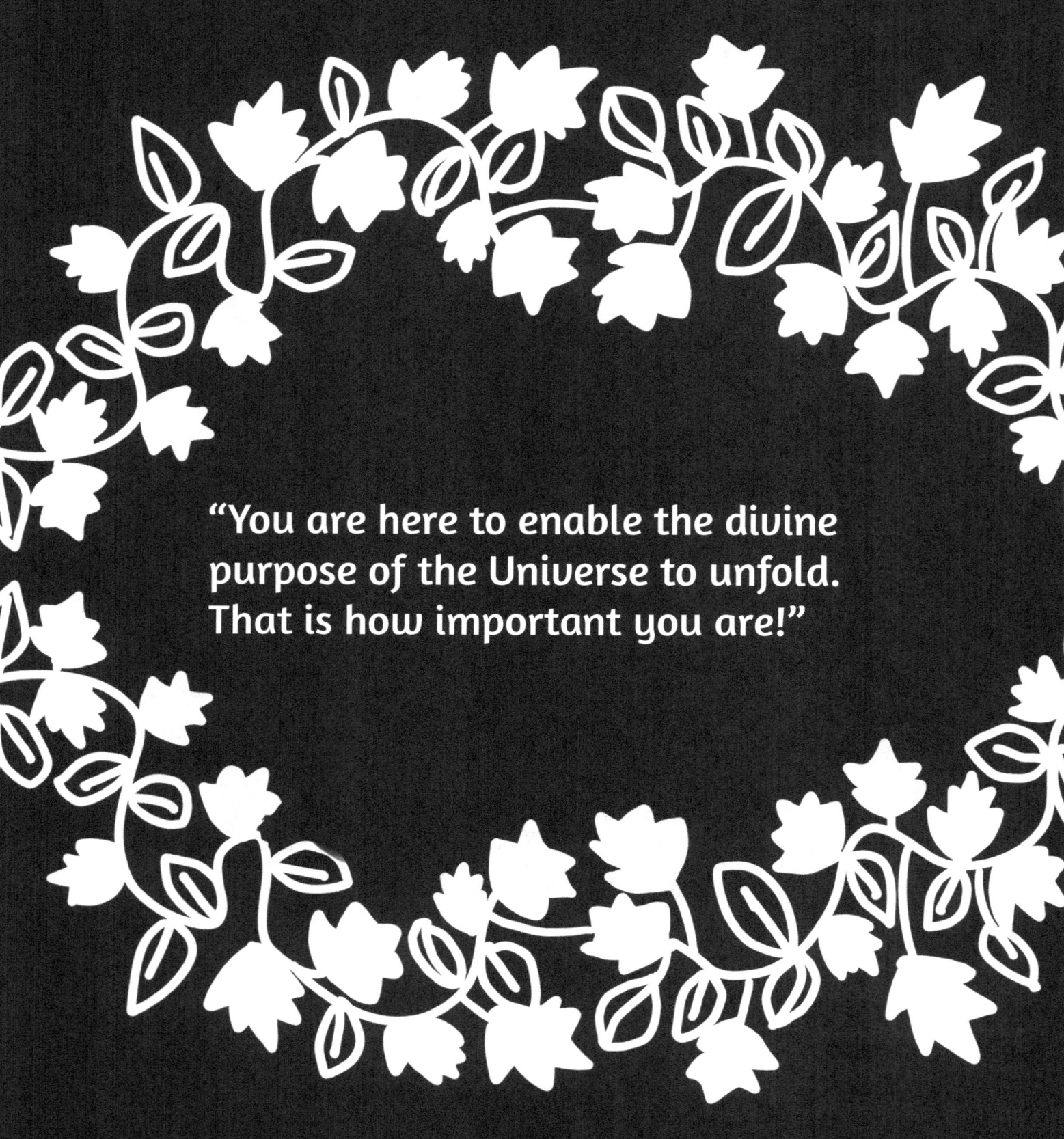

"You are here to enable the divine purpose of the Universe to unfold. That is how important you are!"

Spiritual Chakras

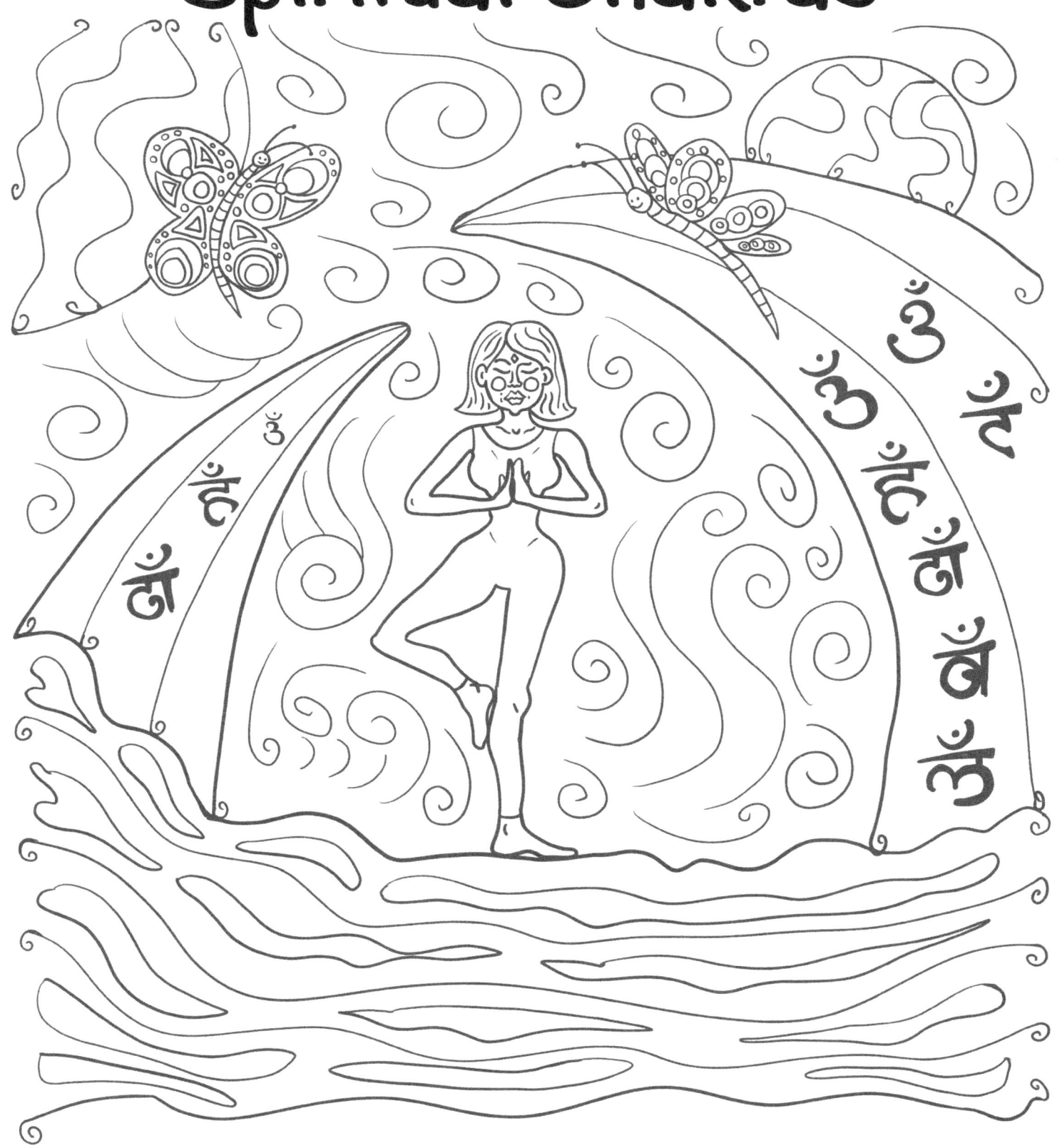

page 65

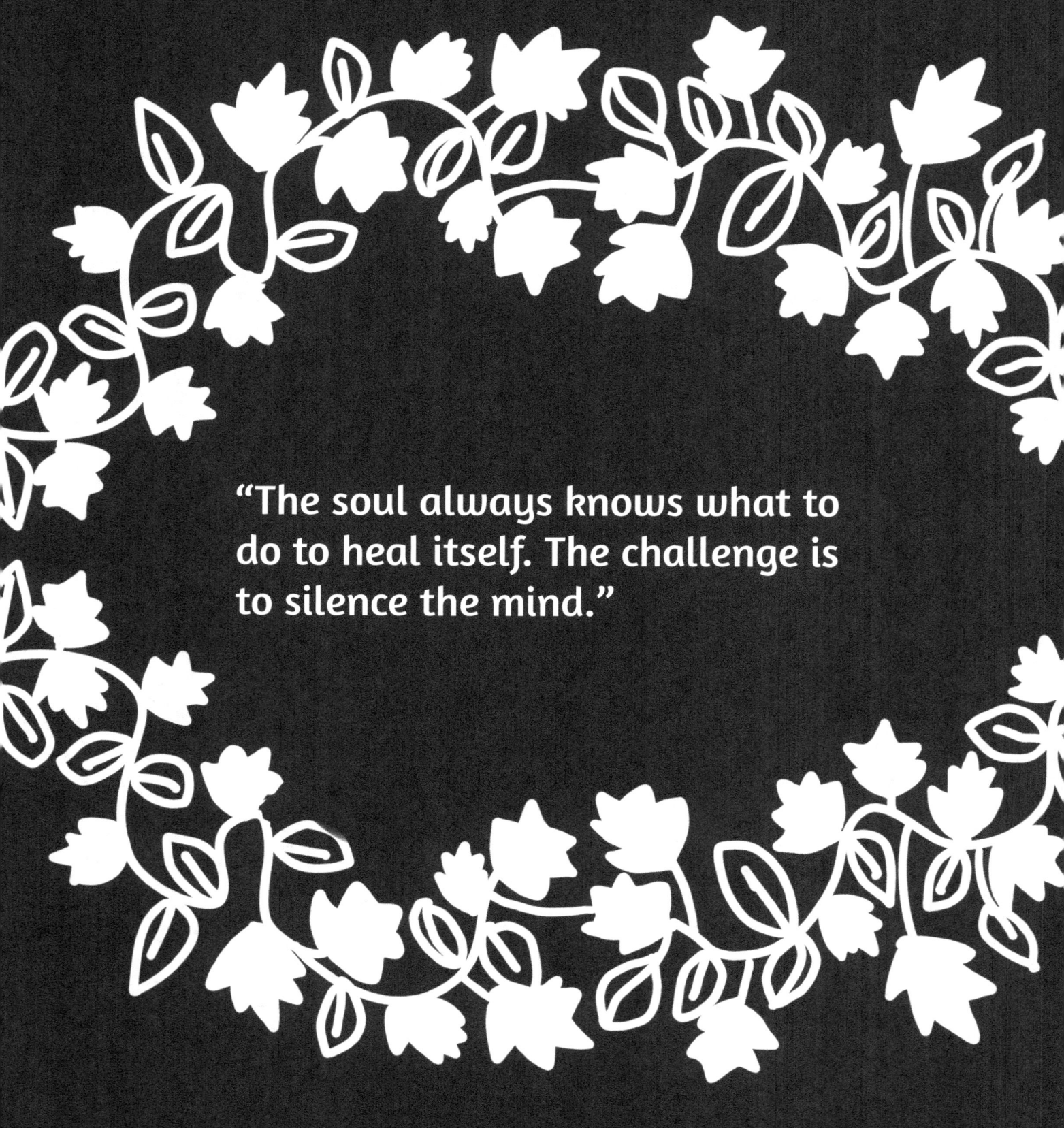

"The soul always knows what to do to heal itself. The challenge is to silence the mind."

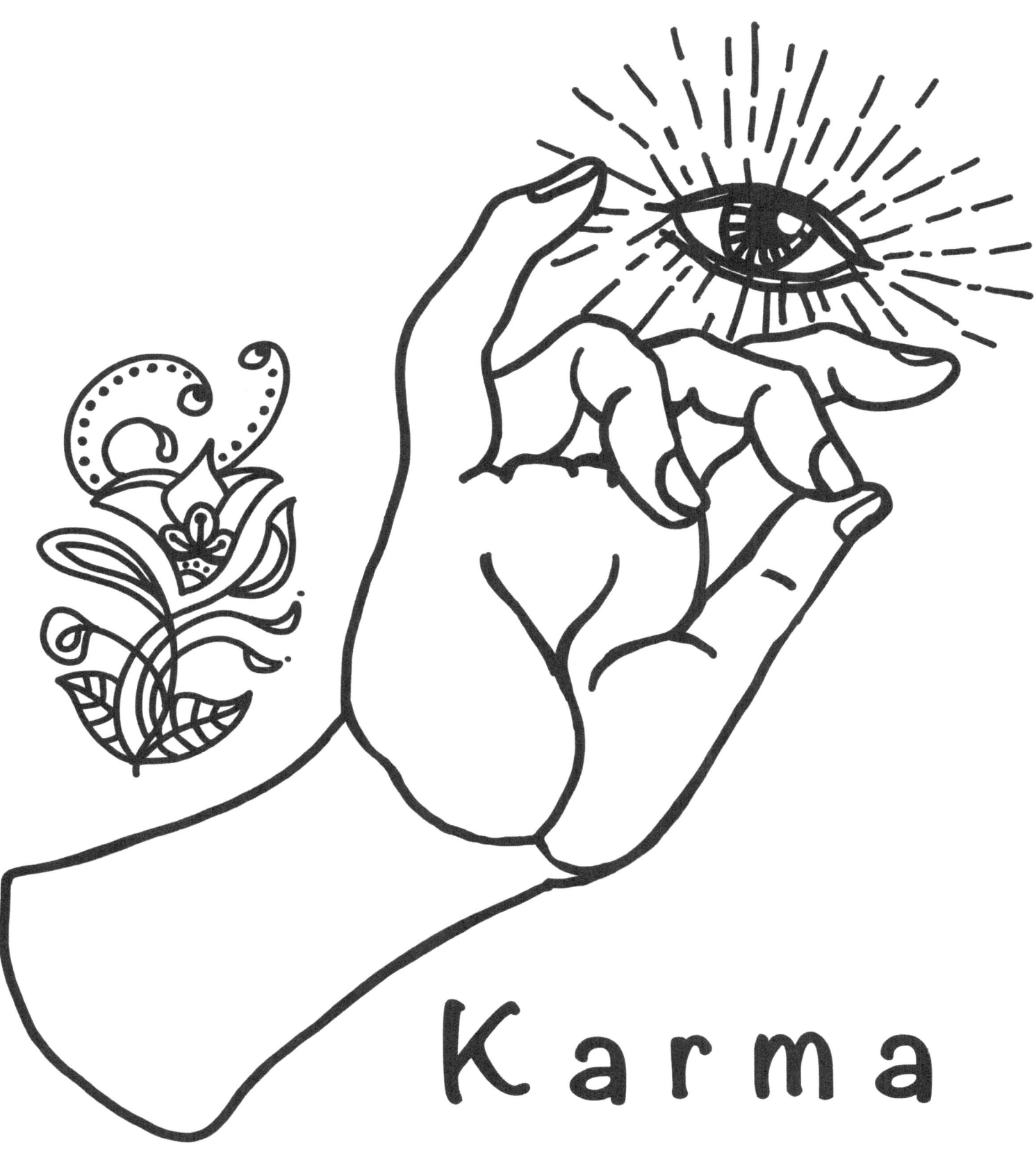

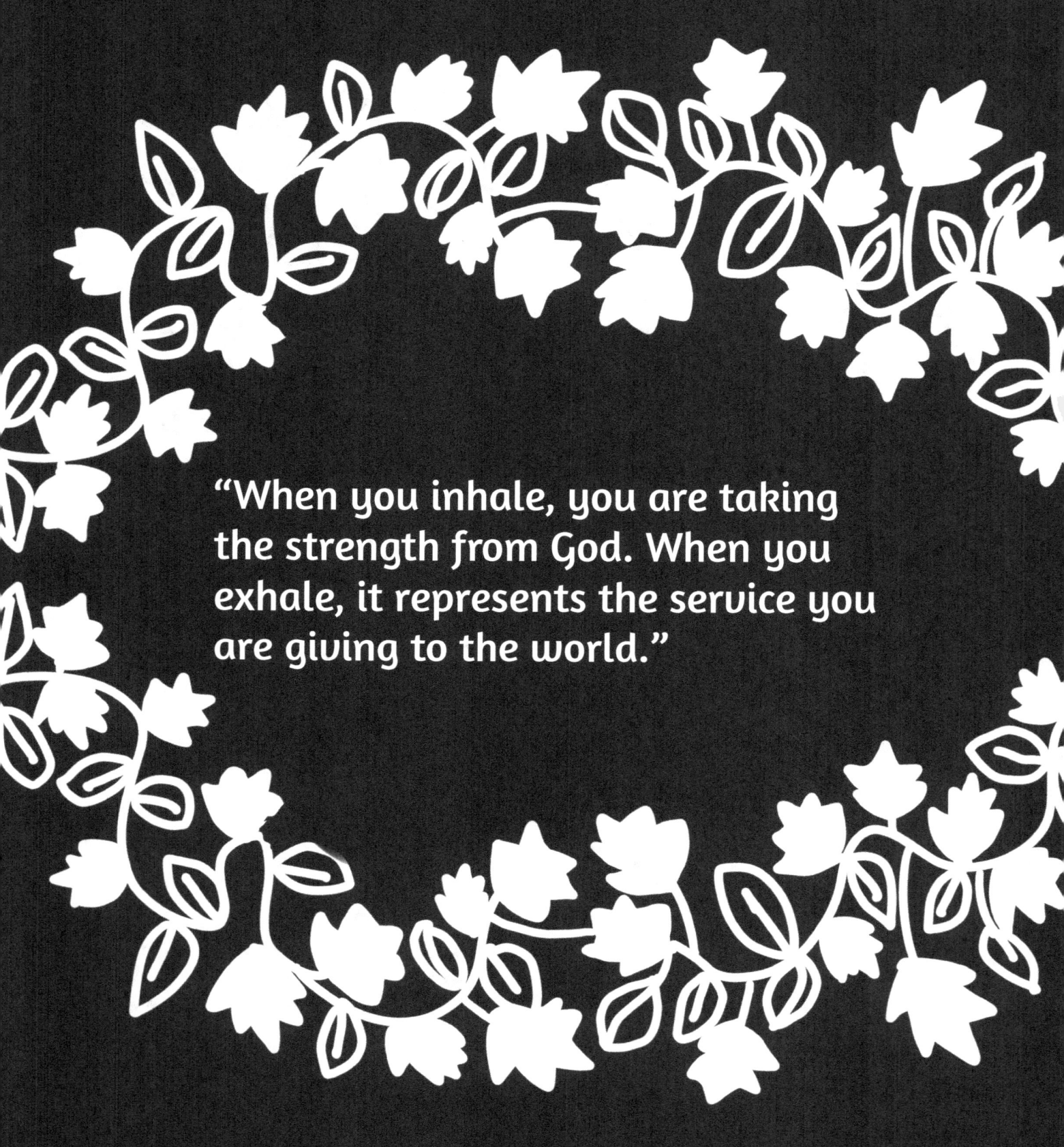

"When you inhale, you are taking the strength from God. When you exhale, it represents the service you are giving to the world."

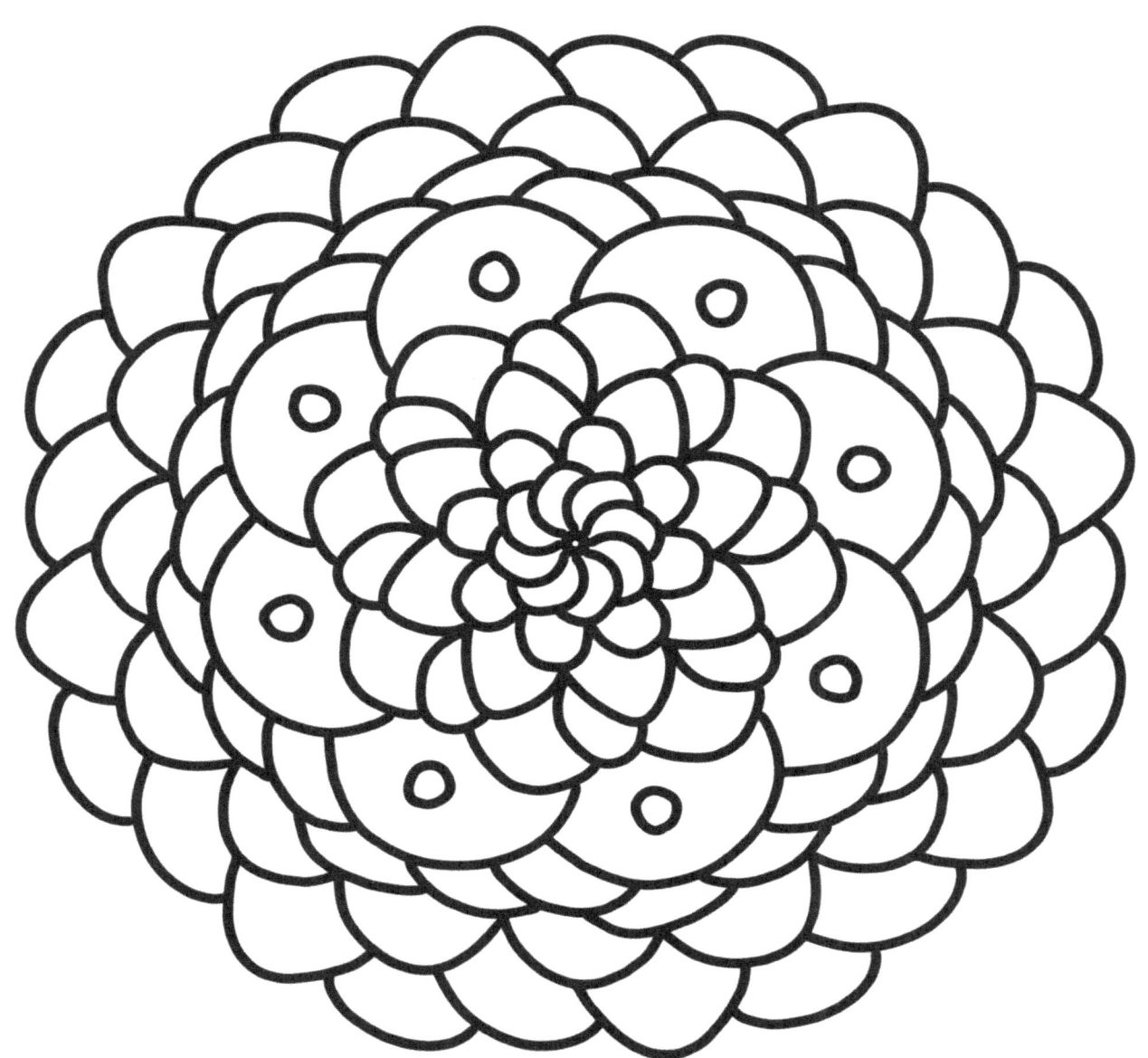

Exhale out

NAMASTÉ: "I bow to the divine in you."

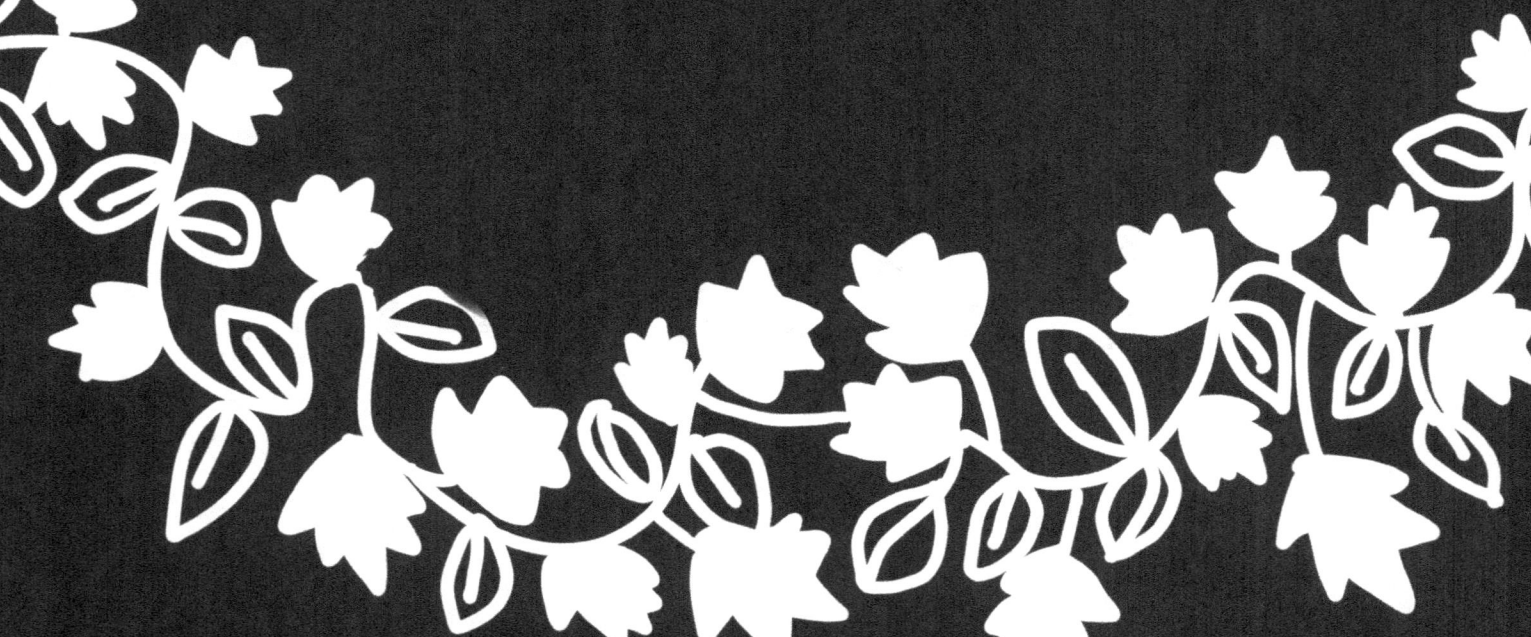

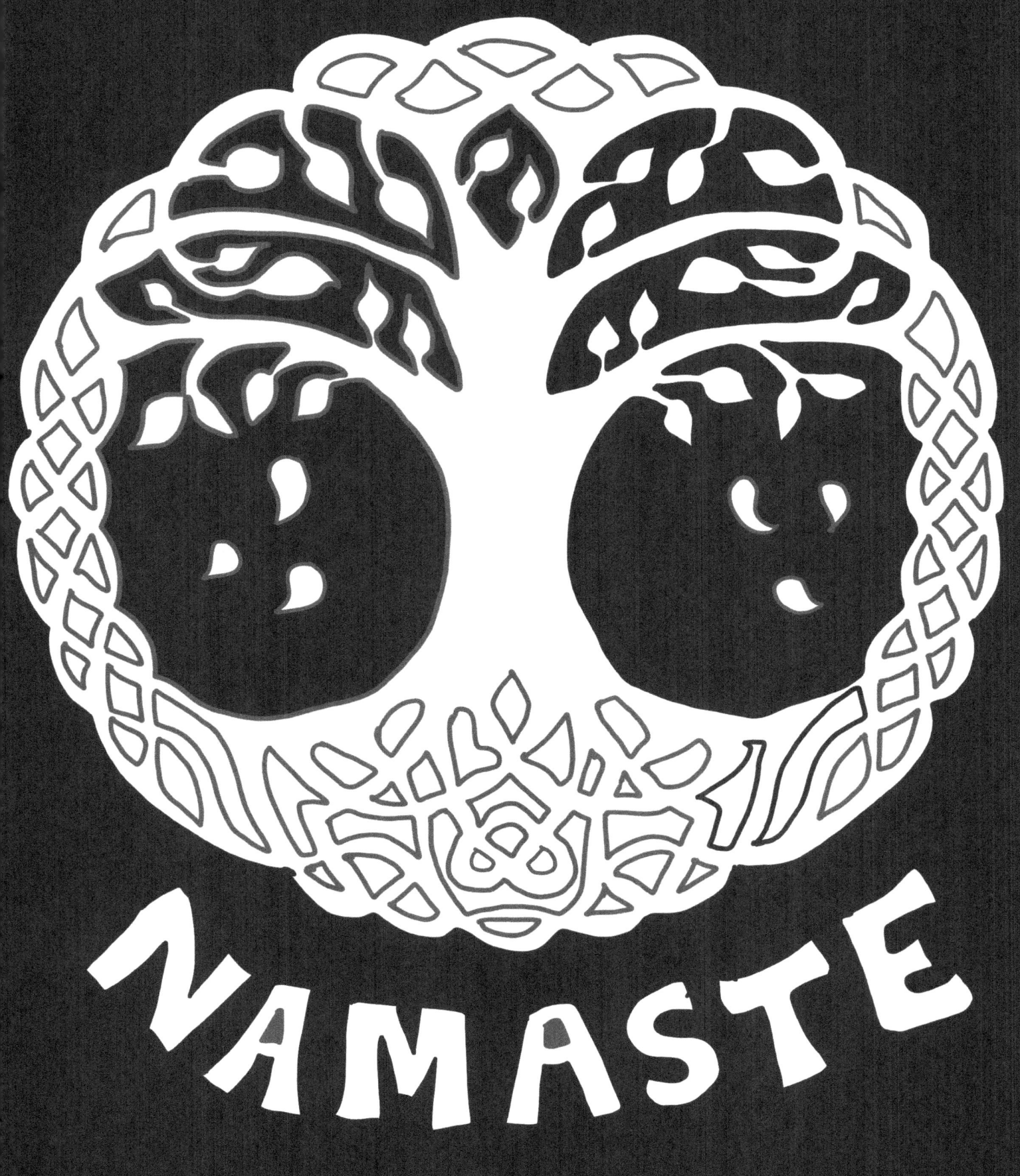

Quote Authors:

- 4. Gautama Buddha
- 6. Soryal Rinpoche
- 8. Mother Teresa
- 10. Yogi Bhajan
- 12. Gautama Buddha
- 14. Geeta S. Iyengar
- 16. Sydney Harris
- 18. Gautama Buddha
- 20. Rodney Yee
- 22. Maya Angelou
- 24. Svatmarama
- 26. Brené Brown
- 28. Eckhart Tolle
- 30. Louise Hay
- 32. Steve Jobs
- 34. Tara Fraser
- 36. Mahatma Ghandi
- 38. Gautama Buddha
- 40. Cheryl Strayed
- 42. Steve Jobs
- 44. Michelle Obama
- 46. Rumi
- 48. Greta Thunberg
- 50. Yogi Bhajan
- 52. Dalai Lama
- 54. Sakyong Miphan
- 56. Oprah Winfrey
- 58. Jigar Gor
- 60. Kripalvananda
- 62. Virginia Woolf
- 64. Eckhart Tolle
- 66. Caroline Myss
- 68. B.K.S. Iyengar
- 70. NAMASTÉ – (nah-mas-tay)
- 72. Amit Ray

www.ingramcontent.com/pod-product-compliance
Lightning Source LLC
Chambersburg PA
CBHW080522220526
45465CB00006B/2565